Uber Driver Road Encounters Series 2

Artwell Dhliwayo

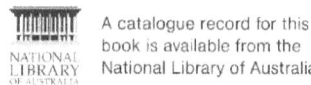
A catalogue record for this book is available from the National Library of Australia

Copyright © 2020 Artwell Dhliwayo
All rights reserved.
ISBN-13: 978-1-922343-25-3

Linellen Press
265 Boomerang Road
Oldbury, Western Australia
www.linellenpress.com.au

Foreword

And COVID-19 Kicks In.

I just returned from a UK tour holiday. The main priority was to polish up the final draft of Uber Driver Series 2. I finished the draft and send it for verification/proofreading by the publishers. While I waited, COVID-19 broke out, bringing an immediate stop to my driving as the scary news spreads like veld fire.

What do you do then? Stop the publishing process or just continue? My gut feeling tells me just to continue. COVID-19 has brought almost everything to a standstill. I may not continue with Uber driving given the current environment. Everything is scary and uncertain. No one is moving around – no functions – no get-togethers – no weddings – no nothing!

To prepare myself for the next series, on the second week of the COVID-19 lockdown, I took a two-hour tour drive of my city, just to survey and see for myself the state of my everyday popular places. I drove everywhere people usually gather in big numbers. It was a horror: surprising, shocking and a very scary drive.

In Perth, the normal high concentration of people is in Fremantle, City Centre, Northbridge, West Leederville, Kings Park, Subiaco, and the Crown Casino. So these were my target drive points on this discovery trip.

Throughout this city and all the popular precincts, there

was nothing. Dry, abandoned and ghostly. Here and there a few takeaway shops were open, one or two people scattered about standing way apart from each other, abiding by social distancing rules. Throughout the city, a few pushbikes, motorbikes and small cars delivered food. This must have been companies like Uber Eats, Deliveroo and Menu Log playing their part to keep life going.

No people, no cars. It was a quiet and ghostly look and feel. The final shock was at the Crown Casino. Throughout the years of my driving, I've been to that place so many times. I've been there literally every hour of the day. The place is always packed with people and cars. At night it is very difficult to find parking. On this day when I arrived, it was deserted, quiet, no people, no cars, nothing. Traffic bollards at the entrance stopped any movement into the Casino driveway. Unbelievable!

A few skeleton staff cars parked in a corner, the whole open space, usually a full car park, was now empty, quiet, nothing, no one!!

It shook me; it frightened me. I got scared and hit the road for home. The two-hour trip gave me an insight into the scale of the COVID–19, its effects on us, on the social fabric and its possible change to the way we live in the future. When all is back to normal, I don't plan to drive anymore, but I must write my final Series 3 giving full details of my lonely trip when COVID-19 kicked in. For now, enjoy Series 2. Series 3 will be coming soon as a round off on how COVID-19 disrupted my driving and source of extra earnings, the impact it had on our way of life and how we moved on.

Contents

Foreword iii
Contents v
Acknowledgments vii
Life as an Uber Driver 1
- View from a distance 2
- As a job 3
- Picture this real story 6
- Driving Pull and Push Factors 8
- Doing something for a long time 12
- Many Players 13
- Pushed to the limit 17
- Driving times 21
- The nasty bits 23
- The risky bits 27
- Personal advantage 29

Story of the Accident 35
The Plain Clothes Police 44
The Free Long Ride 48
Maccas Chicken Nuggets 58
The Brazilian Bush Party 64
The Byford Country Club 68
The Rider Drives 71

Oops!! Wrong crowd	75
Dead Drunk	80
The Responsible Citizen	83
The Annoyed Girlfriend	85
The Gilmore College Student	90
FIFO Got Dumped	93
The Spiked Drink	96
Let's Keep it Professional	100
Unique Lifestyle	106
What Do I Do Next?	110
Retired at Last	115
The Young Electrician	120
The Booze Bus/The Sober Driver	123
Nice People Out There	128
Lady Misses Her Flight	131
Goodbye Sweetie	134
Limping on the Road	138

Acknowledgments

There we go, the second book, Series 2. Many thanks to my wife Felicitas for her support and encouragement and the proof-reading task taking it to the next level, little things we take for granted, the sweetness of family. Again, hats off to you, my pillar. Sorry for the push, but in the end, here we are. God bless.

To my sons, Rufaro and Munya: Rufaro, for sitting with me and peeping into the draft while I corrected mistakes noted by the proofreader – a great bundle of joy, annoyance, and encouragement. My elder son, Munya, a distant supporter of the project. Good on you, son.

To all my siblings all over the world for continuous phrases of encouragement on the project, a very good motivational push through WhatsApp chats. Thank you all.

Life as an Uber Driver

This is no case of reinvention of the wheel. It is a question of innovation with a twist. This mode of transport has existed all over the world for years. We have all seen and used it. Hence the life of the driver behind the scene is nothing new but a new version of the yesteryear figure.

Today the new taxi system merging as Uber is driven by almost anyone – everyday people driving to and from work, or out for a drive anytime someone has free time.

The driver starts and stops anywhere, anytime. How good is that!

The main requirements are a near-new car, more than four years' driving experience, a clean driver's licence and police report, a health clearance and the car certified to be fit to transport people for a fare. This is done by both a private inspector and the government Department of Transport.

Above all this, the car must always be under the control of a sober driver. This, apart from it being an Uber requirement, is common sense for anyone providing such a service to be fair to fellow citizens who are paying to be transported around and would expect to be driven by a sober and responsible person.

It is more fun if one is driving on a part-time basis. This will put less pressure on the driver in terms of rushing for pickups and drop-offs followed by another wave of 'rush' for the next ride prospect.

When one is doing it full-time, there are a few surprises in that operation.

You will come to experience and know that driving can be painful. Usually, it is back pain caused by sitting for extended periods and the prolonged direct contact with the seat; also the hands in continuous control of the steering wheel, and the body and legs in long term contact with parts of the car. It is just unavoidable and very uncomfortable.

The job calls for long hours of driving or on duty to be able to make a decent living. It is a clear case of no pain, no gain.

Uber drivers are not employees; hence you earn what you work for and that is true. So, you drive when you want and stop when you want and that is equally proportional to what your earnings will be. It is a real job that demands a fair bit of your time and dedication to breakthrough.

Several costs are waiting for you along the way, and you should factor these as you go.

View from a distance

The taxi industry is well known everywhere in the world. What taxis do does not need a lecture. It is known. No-one has ever been worried to think about what the drivers do on the road or what they are making. The common thing has been that 'taxis are expensive'.

Then Uber came into play and all eyes are scrutinising what they do. It is the taxi car as we have known it for years. The only difference is it is coming in a new, redesigned package.

Technology has resulted in the birth of this new

package taxi type. The main new features are that the driver is the owner of the car; that same car is used for both your own private business and the Uber for a fare; the car is not marked, and the rider must check the registration plates when the car arrives. It is flashy looking, easy going, and it has a newer and modern feel.

Apart from that visual outside glory appeal, Uber has several needs and requirements that can discourage people from signing up as new drivers and push people away from driving for the public. The best driving times are antisocial hours – that is, you have to be on the road most of the time. That on its own is a negative aspect of the job as you cannot be with family, friends, and relatives at core moments such as mealtimes.

As much as you may have the choice to drive any time, common family times are the popular business peak times.

As a job

The original design of Uber driving is to have individuals register their cars to partner up with Uber and not to be employed by Uber. This justifies the reason why Uber is always advertising for drivers. They want as many people as possible to be registered as drivers. If there are many registered vehicles, it becomes easy and convenient for riders to have cars come to them quickly as there is always one nearby.

As drivers have the flexibility to drive when it suits them, having many registered vehicles ensures there is always a car somewhere near you.

With the changing economic situations of many countries, there has been a direct effect on people's lives. Companies close, merge, change business strategy or reduce the number of people employed. Such actions have seen a lot of people lose jobs or simply be made redundant as companies restructure. Such sudden changes have seen people signing up with Uber and do the driving full-time.

This move will require the driver to be on the road for long hours if one is to make a decent weekly income. When one takes the driving to full-time the true reality of the demands of the job surfaces. The original easy-going perception vanishes. No more casual approach, now the driver must chase peak business periods, morning and late-night, airport runs, and strategically position themself in busy areas.

The long drives and the large number of people getting in and out of that Uber car rears its ugly head. Fatigue kicks in with the long hours on the road. Long-time sitting and controlling the car affects the neck, back, legs, eyes, arms, and the waistline locks due to that prolonged sitting position.

On the vehicle itself, there are on the road damages from minor accidents, scratches, and normal wear and tear. The vehicle will need a fuel top-up every day. Then there is the regular maintenance to keep the vehicle in perfect condition.

If you drive your car to and from work every week, those daily kilometres will add up and the car will be back for service in quick time.

If you are a full-time Uber driver, those kilometres will be covered in a fortnight. This means the car must be serviced twice every month. This is just a service, and does not factor in repairs or ongoing minor damages.

Then there is insurance. This is special insurance for vehicles transporting people for a fare. The vehicle also must be inspected for it to be authorised to use it for that purpose, for public safety's sake.

For the fares paid out to the driver, the government has stretched out its long arm, and they want GST paid out from the very first dollar you make. This is a very unfair game. The common rule is that business pays GST only if it makes over $75,000 a year.

The game has been changed only for Uber.

All these above are a direct cost to the driver which leaves a meagre amount for the driver to live on. This is the real pressure on the driver once one decides to go full-time. Above all, you are a contractor: you earn what you work for, you pay your taxes and then pay yourself.

It is doable to drive full-time, but far from easy. Most people do it for a short while as they run around finding another alternative full-time occupation. A few are locked into Uber because of circumstances. Some people lose jobs and find it hard to get another one, and with age, it may be hard to try to go back to retrain in a new profession. When older people are made redundant, they face problems like competing for jobs with younger people as employers are keen to take younger ones who are cheap and will have more years in the company than older people.

Hence such people will find themselves locked up with Uber earning very little as the bulk of the money goes to the costs of keeping the car on the road.

Like most things people do, there are factors that drive us to do stuff. As you go on, other factors may heavily discourage your strive to keep going.

The need to survive and the obvious duty to provide a service are some of the primary driving factors in Uber driving.

Picture this real story

I was in Fremantle one night, this part of Perth being a hot night out precinct for the young. One young man brought me a good surprise. As I recall this young man must have been a typical *FIFO* (Fly-in-Fly-out) worker, now on his scheduled days off.

Late at night, he sees some homeless person in the street. This person has with him a shopping trolley full of all sorts of things: clothes, small boxes filled with things, a few plastic bags with things, shoes, empty bottles, some blankets, sticks, and other various items, all filthy and carelessly heaped in the shopping trolley.

On top of that, this person was dirty, intimidating and unkempt.

What did the young man do?

He rang Uber to come to pick up that person.

So, the call came to me and straight away I proceeded to the pickup location. On my arrival, I saw exactly what I described above.

The young man who ordered the Uber also stood there. I saw the luggage piled up in the trolley and came out of the car to inspect.

The young man with all his confidence and eagerness to help said to me, "You have to take this man wherever he wants to go, and I will pay for the transport. You can kindly do that for me, right?" He stood there looking straight at me as he dished out the authoritative instructions.

I glanced at the person and could see his unwilling face as he kept a grip on the shopping trolley piled with his belongings.

I made a quick assessment of the job at hand and knew

it was beyond me. My car was too small to fit in all the items. Apart from that, the purpose of Uber is to transport people, not moving people and their belongings.

I suggested to him that he called a 24-hour courier service. I then explained why I could not pick the guy up.

He obviously did not agree with my response, but finally accepted my reasoning and I left the scene.

That is one typical incident.

Along the way, some people ride in the car totally drunk. This inebriated state brings with it an assortment of nasty episodes. People in that state are likely to vomit in the car or outside with their heads popping out while the car is in motion. Or with the car stopped and them dangling their bodies outside.

Any of these actions has a degree of chaos with it. In any case, you need to clean up the car. Some are not drunk but just wearing dirty clothes, and even have mud on their shoes. Many people want to eat in the car and that habit leaves a lot of food debris on the floor and car seats. In some cases, the food containers are left behind as well.

Then there is the involuntary habit of riders who fart in the car. This is my worst experience and I hate it! How do you tell them to stop it? Do you ask if it was them who farted? Do you immediately open your windows to allow fresh air to come to your rescue? Do you pretend you smelled nothing?

Then you question yourself: why you are doing such a job? Are there no other better ways of getting an extra income, your self-search?

The car is left in a mess, you are left feeling yukky. With all these activities the car is depreciating fast. The upholstery wears and fades fast. Seats are stained and, in some cases, the stains are hard to remove. The engine and all moving parts of the car are grinding fast. Doors, windows, boot, lights and all electronics are strained beyond engineering specifications. Quick replacement of the car is imminent, which is a big cost that will lead you to question the wisdom of what you are doing.

Driving Pull and Push Factors

This is a brief account of some of the encounters that encourage and those that discourage the thought of Rideshare driving.

When I jump on the road, every day has its surprises waiting. A huge mixture of short trips, long trips, cancellations, praises, and insults are all waiting somewhere during the day.

After accepting a request, the next act is to start driving to the pickup location. Anything can happen on the way while the rider is waiting. It is possible to miss a turn, or face a detour, or get delayed by road construction or incidences.

Any of the above can subject the driver to the receiving end of either a direct verbal attack or negative rating on you. The mental state and mood of the people picked up as riders/customers and enter the car is a huge gamble with life and safety.

There are grumpy people out there, whether by nature or through personal circumstances is unknown to the driver at the time of pick up. There is no known training on how to deal with and handle such encounters. It is a 50% risk-taking exercise. The more negatives one confronts, the more you will grow to dislike the job. Then there are cases of cheeky people who are suspicious that you want to make an extra dollar from them. They are the ones always bugging you on the route you are taking. The doubt is that you are taking a longer route so you get paid more. They also keep an eye on your speed, the slower you go regardless of the regulated speed, again they assume that it is a tactic to be paid more.

The worst are incidences of drunken people holding and touching you, vomiting, continuously breaking wind, fighting, or just being a public nuisance. These are cases that *really* push you to the limit and an ultimate test of your endurance on this type of work. Many occasions we have read about, heard or seen on the news, cases of drivers being attacked. That is real, it can happen when people are drunk. No amount of apology can soothe the hurt and humiliation caused by most of these incidences. It is something anyone must keep in the back of their minds that you are a candidate for any such mishaps.

When you suddenly dislike each other, this is common and near-natural that sometimes someone takes a ride in your car and for some strange reason you instantly dislike each other. The opposite is also very true, someone comes in and suddenly you have a spark. I have struggled to comprehend how that happens. Just like falling in love, it just happens, and you must deal with it.

When you suddenly find yourself surfing on a wrong topic, is another danger to be on the lookout for. From nowhere you can find yourself triggering delicate private matters: religion, politics, love and marriage, death, family matters, occupations or social status. The list goes on and you need to be cautious and avoid them. The danger is triggering emotions, or if you totally disagree with their viewpoint, that will ruin the trip. Think carefully before delving into these topics.

The need for work and to avoid an idle mind pushes one to do this sort of thing. It is not the best thing to just sit and watch TV, Facebook, randomly surf the internet or look at Youtube videos all day. It is not the best option to do nothing while there is a choice to do such a job in your own chosen day and time, hence I decided to keep doing it.

There is also the need for cash. Uber driving guarantees quick cash every week, which is cash extra to your usual main income. Above all, it is good, and healthy to be a busy person. The everyday job leaves me with a lot of extra time; therefore, it is best to use that spare time for such an additional cash-generating activity. When the body is still young, able and willing, it is a good idea to take advantage of these available opportunities.

In the driving process, there are a lot of nice people out there. The usual movement of coming from home to work, and vice versa, going to social places such as to drinks after work or to family get-togethers or going to functions. Countless nice and happy people are encouraging and who make you look forward to keeping driving. Some will even make you feel good or better and that social aspect of driving is a key encouragement to keep doing it. In a few occasions friendship also starts with such nice people which comes up as a plus to the Uber driver.

I have been humbled by some people from well-to-do neighbourhoods with visibly rich lifestyles who are so down-to-earth when driving them around. You arrive at their house and you can see by the place and cars parked out front that your little Elantra is nowhere near their standard. You pick them up and they are so humble and respectful. Any request or instruction they give is delivered in a kind and considerate way. In such instances, you deliver your service freely and aim to be the best that you can. Not because of fear but you are treated in a way that is equivalent to being encouraged and cheered up for what you are doing. Very encouraging people, I love it. That reminds me not to judge people by where they live or how they are dressed – you will be surprised when you come to know them.

Other great moments are when you strike a brilliant conversation with your rider. This always happens. You find yourself getting the best advice or hint or clue or just learning something you never expected. The trip gets too short, and it lightens up your day. I have had a few such on topics like websites, books, self-help improvements and projects to do, hobbies to pursue, DIY ideas on cars and home projects. I always feel good when I strike good topics with riders and learn something for free. What an incentive!

This is my second book, the material in it is a random collection of the people I have driven around. No pressure of studying or gathering what I am writing. The stories are continuous free flow coming to me as I do my job. My main problem is to filter out which ones I don't want to publish. All this is from the joy of interacting and talking to different people as I drive them around Perth Metro. In the process, I keep developing the tactics to notice people's moods and avoid conflict, to let go if they are not in a talking mood and to deliver the best ride experience in the process.

It is a fact that this new generation mode of transport is catching up with everyone. Being part of it is historical. It will be good to always recount, "I was one of the first people to drive for Uber." The movement of people around cities is massive. The demand is going up and up every day as lifestyles change and people catch up with technology. The contribution to this mass movement of people is a pleasure on its own.

The combination of using your mobile phone, your car and your bank, all being synchronised by Uber from some office somewhere to run a small business is mind-blowing. It is a very interesting use of modern technology unfolding right in front of us. It is amazing to imagine that this is business coordination where electronic gadgets are used to get you into a mini-business without an office anywhere. You can cash out some extra money every week, all depending on your effort and time you put into it.

No day is the same. Every trip is different. It has its own makeup, what you experience with one trip is completely different from what you will encounter in the next trip. The takings are not standard. One cannot decide to join Uber driving based on other drivers' daily takings. If you drive every day, takings on different trips are different. That difference is the total surprise package one is bound to face in this type of job.

It is also good to be reminded there are no strict requirements to start driving Uber. All you need to do is to provide the basics: your driving history, how long you have been driving for, your age, condition of the car, and your mental health status. Within a week there would be an extra flow of cash in your bank account. No gender bias, no nothing. Isn't that encouragement enough for many people to jump into the Uber frenzy?

Doing something for a long time

When you do something for a very long time there is a tendency to like it and be good at it. I have been driving Uber for a long time. That gives me a good insight into the driver operation. It gave me the knowledge of the tricks when to drive, where to drive and how long to drive, and the very tricky situations, such as conflicts with riders, misunderstandings, and general frustration.

At times you silently think over why you are doing it, considering all the problems associated with that type of job.

Having done this for a long time I will know when to stop, when to wait, and to control moments of frustration when there are no ride requests.

Sometimes you drive for a drop-off far out of the built-up urban area, to places where you don't get riders on the return trip. The thought of driving back to the city with no rider on board is a common nightmare, and the silent calculation of how much fuel you're wasting compared to how much you have made is usually a put-off. The endurance of waiting after dropping off passengers is another source of frustration. Having done this for a long time I will know when to wait and the amount of time to waste waiting at a spot. That knowledge alone helps to keep you going because you know the peaks and troughs of the game.

Like in any other business, there are costs involved. One cost is fuel, which means every car movement such as a strategic drive to a busy area or straight drive to pick up, there is unavoidable fuel wastage. Any drive without a paying passenger on board is a waste of fuel. The knowledge of driving for a long time gives you the ability to decide whether to drive or to stay put. That would be a significant saving on fuel and wear and tear on the vehicle.

Many Players

In Series One of *Road Encounters*, the one and only main player was Uber. This was the first Ride-share company to hit the streets of Perth, Western Australia, my hometown.

It came with a bang and shook the traditional taxi industry heavily. The immediate cry was foul play.

In response to the cry, the government quickly set up rules and regulations overnight. Uber faced its toughest resentment and resistance but was unstoppable. Fees and new GST regulations were set up to streamline Uber.

Protests by Taxi operators and call for compensation for their loss of investment in Taxi plates were rampant. It caused a lot of fear and uncertainty on both operators and riders. Luckily enough, law and order prevailed in Australia and there were no reported cases of driver kidnap or attack.

During all this, before a known settlement to the dispute had been achieved, more players came into play:

- Shofer
- Didi
- Ola
- Lyft

These are recent new players that have come into play since the publication of Series One.

This is now a case of no return. No amount of resistance is going to stop this new way of life right here with us.

No one can now blame the commotion on Uber. It is a worldwide unstoppable avalanche. The only way to survive in it is to adapt and go with the flow.

The riders/consumers of the product have spoken loud and clear. Everyone wants new, everyone wants to go with the technology flow. No one wants to be left hanging on to an ancient way of doing things.

Your phone in hand, you call for a ride and in minutes someone is there to pick you up and off you go. No cash transaction, all is electronic. Your phone, someone's car, your bank account, done! To continue using the system, you and the driver rate each other after the ride. If you fall below a set star rating, you are out, and you are back to the tradition. Who wants that, hence you both police each other and the system operates and self-manages, and life goes on.

To throw everyone into a total spin, technology has come up with self-drive cars.

Uber is already pioneering this system and sooner or later, Ride-share is everywhere, and self-drive cars will be the thing.

Let's all embrace this transport system and gear ourselves to move with technology as it is inevitable, or else you and I will be totally left behind. Ride-share is the way to go, there is no going back.

As a new technology, everybody wants to use it. This technology is here to stay. The operation of the business is bound to face several legal problems and challenges from other players. The 'riders' who are the major consumers of this business type are keen to use technology. That is a positive to this type of business. Many more competitors are obviously going to emerge, putting the pressure on in terms of price as they scramble for riders.

Regardless of what will happen, this is the future and the only obvious way to go for now. It is no secret that self-drive vehicles are coming. From this, we can foresee the struggle ahead and the heavy competition, demands, and pressure of excessive fees and licences. That cost element will be a dissuading factor for the few loyal hard-working drivers.

Change is imminent and no one can run away from it.

The traditional taxi operators must live with it. This is a common phenomenon in most business operations, industrial, retail and manufacturing. So it is with Uber. As people are on the frenzy of using this service other operators are also coming with the same use of technology hence it is competition on and on.

There is a high possibility that Ride-share companies will be the future of such businesses. Traditional taxi operators will gradually disappear unless they take the new Ride-share technology on board. At the same time, the Ride-share operation will most likely be disrupted when self-drive vehicles come on board. This is a technology already in use in other parts of the world. It is already on trial and sooner or later it will be everywhere just like Uber came, suddenly everywhere. People who own timeshare vehicles are likely to be taken by surprise when the self-drive comes on board.

They will claim to be disadvantaged just like the current taxi operators are up in arms with Uber. People need to keep embracing new technology which is affecting business changes and modes of operations, and one is not likely to be taken by surprise when changes come. A lot of players will be on board since this is public knowledge that Ride-share will be used with driverless vehicles in the future. The current high turnover of staff driving Ride-share vehicles is high on its own. If taxi operators vanish today, Uber on its own is not likely to meet the current transport demands. Most drivers operate on a part-time basis and they are not fully committed as they have jobs elsewhere. This compromises the expected high-quality service and commuters are left stranded when there are not enough vehicles to meet demand at any time.

Pushed to the limit

This is a typical example of some of the incidents that happen which can put you off as a driver.

I was in Southern River one evening and received a rider request call. I glanced at the address: it was in one of the main suburban roads.

Straight away I punched on my GPS and off I went to the pickup point. I was in very good spirits and looking forward to meeting the riders. On arrival, I stopped some distance from the exact place where they might have been standing or waiting. Remember this is a shopping centre – GPS does not pinpoint the exact shop but tells you that you have arrived.

On arrival, I realised it was a small shopping centre and the riders were somewhere within that complex. I stopped and parked near some shops and started looking around for someone who looked like they were ready for a ride.

There was a bar, a restaurant, and supermarket, so I expected the rider to come from any of these three.

I drove past the bar again, past the supermarket and parked in a parking bay next to a gymnasium. After a while, without seeing anyone I decided to give the rider a call and pulled my mobile phone out. As I was just about to press the digits, I saw some people looking at their phone and looking around and I suspected them to be my riders. They spotted the car registration number and started walking towards my Elantra. On their arrival, I opened the doors for them as a courtesy. All three passengers did not look happy. I could tell something was not right.

As I locked in their destination, the place and route came up on the screen. I knew the place and drove straight away at ease. It did not take me long. One lady sat in the passenger seat and the two gentlemen took the back seats. Straight away one of the back passengers said to me, "Why did you stop here?"

I did not have an immediate answer to that question.

Then he goes on again, saying, "We were right there at Dan Murphy, not this f******* place. You just stop anywhere you like ... what's wrong with you?"

Now, this is where you get caught off guard. This was the last thing I ever expected when they came into the car. When I saw them coming and walking fast, I expected to open the doors for them, they come in cheerfully, good greetings and off we go. But then, just look at this start of the trip.

Just picture that starting scene. Where do you start? How do you happily deliver service? How do you have a good small chat along the way? Does this make you look forward to a perfect service delivery? Do you expect to keep doing this? This is the real challenge awaiting you every now and then. How do you prepare yourself for such surprises?

Instead of a happy initial greeting, I was faced with a situation where I was to come up with a perfect answer to the question.

After a brief pause thinking over the question I explained, "That was the address shown on the GPS."

"But that's not where we were standing! Can you not see that on your f****** phone?" barked the man again.

He went on to explain that he was standing next to the bottle shop and he saw me driving past. According to him he had put the right address and expected me to pinpoint exactly where he was standing.

Then he goes on at me again: "If you did not know, why

then did you stop here? If you cannot drive and read maps, then please don't drive!" He stressed the point forcefully.

Instead of taking direct blame on the accusation, I tried to explain the exact pickup point problem. I explained that at a shopping centre with many individual shops along a main road, all will have the one physical address. Say the complex is number 20, then the shops will come up as Units 1, Unit 2, Unit 3, etc. If you are standing at say Unit 2/ 20, the GPS cannot pinpoint exactly where you need to be picked up but it will show you that you have arrived at number 20. In that case, we both must try to see each other. As the driver, I will stop at number 20, as the rider you will walk out of your unit and position yourself somewhere visible so the driver can see you.

The explanation fell on deaf ears. Just after listening for a few seconds as I was talking, the lady sitting at the front rudely interrupted and said, "Just start driving. Let's go … you are now wasting time."

In such moments you feel like giving up. You just run out of energy. It will be a question of keep doing it or not. It is just frustrating.

After I attempted to explain and was not listened to, I started driving and gave up the explanation. This is it: in customer service you must do the right thing, but inside me, I was not happy. I felt wounded. We started the trip on a very bad note. No one was talking. They were visibly angry and had not listened or paid attention to my explanation. We were all quiet in the car for the duration of the ride. I saw the address we were going to, and I was happy we were going to a similar place. That is a mini suburban shopping centre with restaurants, bars, liquor shops, and supermarkets. We were going to one of the bars.

All the way I followed the GPS instructions. And I could see from the lady on the passenger seat that she was also paying close attention to the directions on the GPS. We went in turns and twists, past all the suburban houses and straight up onto the shopping centre. Now this time even the two people sitting at the back of the car all had their eyes fixed on the GPS.

On arrival, I indicated and turned into the shopping centre. I could see the bar where I was supposed to stop and drop them. I knew the place, but I chose to follow the GPS instruction as everybody was watching.

Then the GPS started giving out loud and clear instructions. Turn right, turn left, right again and left. Then announced, "You have arrived."

We were now going past the parking and drop off bays of the bar they were supposed to go to, and everybody could see that we were driving past. That was the moment when the lady sitting at the front said aloud for everybody to hear: "Oh yes, now I see what you meant."

By then the car was about a good distance away from the drop off point. As I stopped the vehicle, I politely said to them all: "This is exactly what happened when I came to pick you up, so you see, this is what I was trying to explain to you."

They just opened the doors and walked away. No goodbye, no nothing, but the lady closed the door, turned her head and said, "Thank you." Then she turned and walked away to join her two mates.

I appreciated her response. At least she knew what I meant earlier when I tried to explain to them at the pick-up point.

I remained sitting in my car for a while. In such moments you can't help the feeling of unworthiness and the need to swallow your pride. Such ridicule will last in you for a long time. You will try to brush it aside, but it will remain hanging in you for a while. It forces you to reconsider to keep doing what you're doing or to stop. What will happen if you flare up in anger and the passenger does the same? In the end, there is a confrontation. Who will be the loser? It will be a case of the service provider versus customer and the service provider will be wrong. It is one of those trips or moments that will throw you out of your comfort zone.

Driving times

Most of the encounters narrated in *Series One* are composed of drives that were done randomly – any time of the day. With more driving experience, I decided to be a night driver, or rather an early morning driver. I've now opted to drive anytime between 2.00 am and 8.00 am. These days I only drive Friday, Saturday and Sunday morning. You, like most people, will be asking the question, "Is that the right time to drive? Are there any people moving during that time?"

Yes, there are people in need of a ride 24 hours a day. At all times someone is going somewhere. Driving during such hours is good and has a lot of positives.

Most of the drives are long, that is, more than 30 minutes. There are few dramas on the road – this means there are fewer encounters with drunkards or people in a disorderly behaviour state. During that time most people are going to the airport, such as FIFO workers. There are also people coming from or going to work. The majority are those coming from private functions in homes or venues or from any sort of night-long sessions. There are fewer chances of disruptive people who can go on and on about minor issues such as the condition and type of the car or the variety of refreshments in the car. High chances are that you just pick up happy people ready to go with the flow and that is the 'positive' about early morning driving.

During those early hours people who got drunk in the early hours of the night will be sobering up and all they want is to go home and sleep. They don't want to talk to anyone, no silly questions, no silly behaviour, just quiet. That is the beauty of driving during those hours.

Also, during that time, the roads are less congested and that gives a happy and easy driving experience. There are fewer chances of encounters with the police on the road. In Western Australia when you are driving around there is a high chance of coming across speed cameras mounted on the roadside.

Like anything else, there is a downside to night driving. The body is designed to sleep at night and work during the day. It is a fact that driving during those hours one is going against natural body function. The body will be tired, and it just wants to go to sleep, so there is an ongoing fight with the body to stay awake. Most times at night I drive with the windows down and the car aircon off. That helps to keep a cool breeze blowing in the car and that will keep me, the driver, awake. Failure to do that, the body will get warm and will go to sleep while driving. That will be a disaster for both the driver and the rider, and that is least expected to happen.

Apart from this wake-up technique, there is also the need to get enough sleep to be able to stay awake when driving during such hours. I'm happy that at the time of writing this, Uber has put in place strict driving times for drivers to follow. This helps in road safety and helps drivers do their jobs efficiently and in good health and spirit. The GPS and the Uber log-in system will lock you out if you drive for more than twelve hours. It is mandatory to rest for not less than eight hours after every shift. This is a good move for both riders and drivers. The drivers will get enough rest and riders will have a healthy, rested, alert driver delivering a safe and reliable service.

The other downside is that the vehicle instruments are on throughout the driving period. That is the aircon is on, the lights are on and the instrument panel is continuously illuminated. In no time there is always a need to replace the globes, and that is a direct cost to the small business.

The nasty bits

There are a lot of incidences that will put you off. In *Series One*, there were a few encounters narrated. That is just a sneak peek of what happens most of the time. There are numerous cases of people kissing or requesting to have sex in the car in your presence as the driver. *No!* is the definite answer but you have to be a diplomatic *No*. We are there to serve and to deliver what has been requested. Such requests are to be rejected. The way you reject and move on is the hard and nasty way. After rejecting such a request, the next thing is to keep watch. You must monitor what is happening in your car to be in control.

Now that brings a compromise to service delivery because you are driving and keeping an eye on the rear-view mirror to monitor anything that is happening in the back seat. It is easy to stop them from having sex in the car, but you can't stop people kissing and it goes on and on and it's a disruption to the driver. Viewing that scenario, you can easily conclude how frustrating it is and your dislike of such encounters.

In *Series One* I gave two good narrations of people vomiting in and outside the vehicle.

Regardless of how much they are going to pay to clean the mess, you are still going to face the consequences of the inconvenience in terms of stopping the operation until the car is ready and clean enough for the next riders.

Then there is the worst case of people breaking wind in the car. I've had several of these incidences. All sorts of people, it is so strange, disgusting and frustrating and you are forced to dislike the person totally.

Like, in this case: one Saturday around 4.30 am I picked up a lady from Fremantle; she was going to Midland. That is a 30-minute trip. She must have been out to a private house function or birthday party or something. I arrived at the place and could see lots of cars outside in the street. A few people were randomly mingling in the yard, smoking and holding drinks. A typical late-night party coming to an end scenario.

She was already waiting by the driveway when I arrived. I stopped the Hyundai Elantra, she quietly hopped in, and we took off. A young, decent-looking lady just tired and wanting to go home, but a bit tipsy I could tell from her line of communication. A short time into the drive she fell into a deep slumber. I could see her head dropping, and her ongoing attempt to lift it to look like she was not dozing. The head kept dropping, typical of a deeply asleep drunken person in a sitting position. I let her sleep with soothing music playing as I drove to her intended destination.

Then she lets one out. I'm telling you; you don't want to be there – it was a horrible pungent smell. Immediately I had to open the windows to let the fresh air in. As the cold breeze blew into the car she instantly woke up. I'm pretty sure she then noticed what she'd just done. Straight away with that, she knew why the windows were wide open in the cold of the early morning. There was no question to ask since we both knew the reason.

These bodily discharges are surely meant for private experiences. It's strange enough how unbearable it is if it's not yours and how everything is disgusting around you and how you dislike the person who has just done that. Unfortunately, this happened about three times throughout the journey. Each time I had to lower the windows. She would wake up, adjust her sitting position and rub her feet on the floor, pretending nothing had happened.

We both felt the uncomfortable situation in the car, and that's how the trip went. By the time we arrived at her destination, I was sick of it but could not escape the horrible subjection. Only that dreadful smell and dislike of the whole trip. You can imagine that long drive experience. You are subjected to such a horrible smell, you don't like it, you can't question the person; you just have to live with it; deal with it. That's a classic nasty bit of this type of job.

Same story to the other early morning drive when I picked up an elderly couple from the Crown Casino to Canning Vale. Another classic 30-minute drive subjection to revulsion. I picked them up, a very cheerful couple who got in the car and quickly narrated to me their casino experience of the night. How they came and had fun but lost a fair bit of money. To console themselves they spent the last three hours drinking any alcohol of their choice regardless of price. At the end of the day, they were just happy and laughing about it.

Again, a short distance into the drive the man was lumped on the seat, eyes closed, mouth ajar and a slight snore. I could see him dropping on and off on his back-seat position through my rear-view mirror. I kept talking to the wife for a while, she also looked tired, but she did not succumb to the call to sleep.

With about five kilometres to their destination, the man let out a nasty pong in his sleep. That loud horrible and disgusting sound that no one can miss or hide. The poor wife sitting beside him just let out this surprised sound to try to cover up. At the same time, she gave him a friendly shake to wake him up. She could not do anything to hide the stench the husband had just released.

In a very short space of time, the smell filled up the car. Immediately, without much thinking about it, I lowered the windows as the heavy obnoxious gas overpowered us all. The man shrugged himself up and pretended nothing had happened, but we all knew. An air of embarrassment kept us all quiet.

These are some of the incidences that will make you think twice or regret doing what you are doing. You question yourself why you are doing that, and why you are subjecting yourself to such unpleasant, disgusting and humiliating exposures. Surely there must be other better ways of making an extra dollar.

It is clear and honest to say that these experiences are a small fraction of the whole job. Not every day is like that, there are many more fun experiences which will override these minor incidences. The love and joy of what you are doing is the major drive force behind it. The longer you do it the easier you will accept it as how it is and just move on.

What number of stories and incidences we can get from Taxi drivers who have done this type of job for most of their lives, but never put anything into writing?

Regardless of who has seen and done what in the past, such nasty bits and experiences will stay in your head and affect your everyday experience and vision, and the possibility of fear and dislike of people.

The risky bits

One major fearsome and risky bit in this job are strangers in the car. You are bound to have people you would have never been associated within your daily life. All sorts of characters, personalities, ages, races, etc., are your customers. It is not your job to select who you want or do not want in your car. Every call that comes, your number one responsibility is to accept it and go right away to pick them up. You will discover all about them when you get there. Their appearance and presentation you will see a minute before they sneak into your car, that's it. No room for assessment and selection. That time frame will not give you the chance to decide either to pick them up or reject. You are there, you just must pick them, unless there is a reason beyond reasonable doubt.

The fact is that you don't know who they are. You don't know the purpose of the trip, you don't know what they are carrying, you don't know their background, you know nothing about them. It is very possible that by giving them a ride, you can be facilitating a crime. You can be helping someone flee from or go to a crime scene, you just don't know!

At the same time, high chances are that you are doing the right thing, you are helping people in urgent business need of such transport. Somewhere people cannot drive themselves and will need that service. Good citizens are always in need of such a service. Most of the time, you will be doing the right thing, the service is required and applauded by the community.

That will be the good part. It is only appalling when you realise you are being used for evil acts and purposes, but you did it unknowingly. Only the bad elements in the community will bring the risky and nasty bits in providing such a service, and that will make you sick when you think that you are doing the right thing, but only to realise that you are helping people with bad intentions. Petty and seasoned criminals, robbers and habitual law violating citizens bring a wicked reputation to the service and these are some of the nasty bits in this type of job.

Another element of nastiness in this job is the road itself. The road has been a major hazard and life-threatening to each one of us. If your job involves being on the road every day for the minimum eight hours of your workday, you can imagine the degree of danger your life is exposed to.

There is a possibility of death and injury any minute in the duration of your duties. There are countless road mishaps from driver errors, technical errors, and anything else that can cause incidence and accidents on the road. Other drivers who can be tired, misjudgment and failure to control the vehicle, young and less experienced drivers, road conditions, weather conditions and anything else on the road.

The high degree of risk is right in your face for the entire duration of your duty.

Abuse, ridicule, and humiliation on the road is another silent major thing that is not discussed much, but it's very common on the road. Road rage, insults from other road users and bullying on the road are all cases of the nasty bits.

Each time you are on the road you are dicing with life

and safety. On the road, you are exposed to instant death and harm. Survival is by chance and luck. It is a 50% chance, but most people out there are good, it is the unruly fraction that puts everyone at risk.

In general discussion with most riders, they always confess they are not comfortable or will never be willing to do such a job. The thought of having a stranger in your car and driving them around is risky. I have encountered riders who look very fierce and picking up people at very odd hours of the day going to very dubious places. You just leave everything to luck and fate. What will happen will happen. Just keep hoping that nothing bad will happen, and that is the nasty bits in this game.

Personal advantage

You acquire general knowledge while doing this job – knowledge of the place you live, that is, the city you are living in – knowledge of driving, apart from just moving the vehicle – knowledge that the road is a shared space. The knowledge to interact with people, to respect people, not to judge people, and generally to give people their own space.

There is also the general knowledge of running a small business. The responsibility to collect money, set aside some for yourself and to allocate for expenses and to pay your taxes. It is not something you can know if you are not doing it practically, that activity goes a long way into general knowledge bank.

As you live in your city, there are places you will never know if you just drive from home to work every day. You need reasons to drive to some places to see them. It may not be necessary knowledge, but it is a plus in your general knowledge bank.

Cities are intricate places that you love to know more about. There are intricate road networks such as flyovers, bypasses, tunnels, and major roads and intersections. These are known by everyone in the city, but the more you drive around you will know of laneways, bypasses, free and quick parking spots, especially behind major buildings. Venues like concert halls, sports stadiums, theatres, town halls, are sometimes tricky to navigate to. You will be surprised to know that those places are all designed with entry and exit points. The general public will never know all this unless someone uses them regularly. It is always a pleasure when picking up people or dropping them off at such places and you expertly navigate and people are always very surprised and impressed about how you know all that. That is another plus to the general knowledge you acquire when doing such a job as you deliver customer satisfaction.

There is also free knowledge of world geography. This is something you get by developing an interest in people. You will notice that you come across so many people from different parts of the world. Just by asking them questions and talking to them, you will end up knowing where they come from. From your own personal interests, you may end up looking on maps and learn and know lots about world geography. For instance, you are in Australia, you drive someone from Brazil, Japan, the Middle East, Europe or from Africa. If you have interest after the discussions in your own time, you can always check map reference where these places are, and you will learn about them.

I have personally enjoyed studying the Caribbean region and all the islands around that area after driving someone from Jamaica. I have also had the pleasure of studying and understanding the Asia region. I have come to know most of the countries, some of which I might have never bothered, but because I have spoken to someone from that region, I became interested to know the real geographical position. It is free knowledge – only an individual's interest is required to get it. If you look and have the desire, you can learn a lot in the process.

When I am driving someone from some place I've never been, I'm always keen to later check on google the geographical position of their country of origin and study it. But then when you google those places you end up studying the adjacent areas; in most cases, you are surprised what you see and a good surprise in what you didn't even know. Things like capital cities and countries, sharing borders, rivers and lakes, the seas and oceans nearest to such places. It is just a free general knowledge you get if you have the will. I love it and I've acquired a lot of world geography knowledge through it.

Another thing you learn for free is the art of communication. Interaction with people teaches you many things. You learn to respect people's views; you also learn to give people their own space. Sometimes people just don't want to talk, sometimes they don't like questions – these are some of the things you learn along the way. The art of judgment of when to talk, when to throw in a joke, and to read people's moods is very important. You will also learn not to judge people until you really know them. People are an interesting observation, in a country like Australia you cannot judge people by their dressing, how they travel, even where they live. In most cases you will be surprised who people are, what they do, where they have been; you will be surprised when you come to fully know if you strike the chance to talk to them.

As I spent most of my time on the road, I have obviously become a better driver. The term 'better driver' can be too broad, but this is the ability to be professional on the road. There are a lot of activities on the road. There are lots of distractions, also lots of anger and frustrations. No one will ever know what people are going through, what is in people's heads, that is, what people are thinking, what they are going through, or even what happened just before they came to be in control of the vehicle. If you do not consider all these things, you will end up in road rage through minor conflicts. It is important to know that a vehicle is a lethal weapon with a spiral effect if we don't handle it properly.

The anticipation and look out for all sources of distractions and reactions will help to become a better driver. The knowledge of the road as an entity on how to handle it goes a long way. The road has rules and regulations. If these are properly followed by looking as you drive, reading and following the instructions, anyone is bound to enjoy any form of driving anytime. Having spent considerable time behind the wheel, and at one time driving full-time, that has given me full advantage to know the road better and to be a better driver.

It is important to know that the use of the road is not just the ability to set the car in motion. I become a better driver in terms of being law-abiding, maintaining the speed limits and avoiding accidents at all costs. It is like an extension of defensive driving, and that is for your benefit and the good of other road users as well.

In the process of driving, you will learn of certain professions, activities, hobbies and small cash-generating ideas from talking to people. You will be amazed how much information and ideas people can give you for free.

This sounds unrealistic but it is very true, people have lots and lots of information, ideas, and suggestions. All that is required is to master the art of communication, listen and manipulate people into talking the correct subject lines.

I have driven musicians, artists, professors, government office workers, pilots, doctors, lawyers, all sorts of tradespeople in fly-in-fly-out, in both technical and administration positions. It was interesting to drive seamen, stevedores, undertakers, medical professionals, business executives, entrepreneurs, and lots of small business operators.

A few of my most interesting rides have been with my neighbours. I have driven a few people in my street. It has always been a surprise ending up in laughter and a very good and happy ride as they get surprised when I pitch up at their driveway and they discover that their very street neighbour is now their driver. Always an interesting discovery to them.

Uber driving is a small business. When one is contracted to come on the platform, you come in as a contractor. This means you will be running a small business entity. As small as it is, cash is generated. Money flows into your bank account every week. This leaves you with the obligation to account for the money for yourself, for the expense of the business, and tax purposes either every three months or at the end of the year.

As you do this, you learn business management at a micro-level. That sense of responsibility and personal drive can be translated to do a bigger business activity. Hence, it is a free business lesson as you go. No one is there to tell you when to go drive or when to stop. It is an internal personal drive. In a short space of time, you can be your own judge to see if it is something for you. There are no huge sums of money that flow into your account any day. It is little amounts that add up. The vision of that 'adding up' process and the payment of expenses, and good customer care, and being law-abiding as stated by the government and by the company. That is the free lesson you will learn as you drive.

The best part every week is to see some cash in your bank account. It is always interesting to keep the mind busy by doing something outside the main job. Apart from the expenses and the possibility of nasty encounters on the road, it is interesting to do some cash-generating activities. If you are driving part-time it may not be much, but that little bit will cover daily expenses such as fuel, going out for drinks after work or family outing activities. The more you do it, the more you can be able to pay for bigger expenses.

Driving for Uber has helped me to keep my mind busy on my regular workday off, or short holidays. There is always some driving to do and the mind is never idle, and that is good for my soul. The question of how much you make is secondary to me.

Story of the Accident

I had picked up one of my regular clients from Perth domestic airport, going to Byford. I had driven this guy for a long time, and we were very close, being from the same suburb and having known each other for a while. We left the airport, drove down Tonkin Highway towards Armadale (southbound). As we cruised down past the new airport spaghetti junction and under the Roe Highway overpass, the road was just busy, a typical Friday afternoon. I was on the outer left lane and going at the zone regulated speed of 80 km/hr. We were relaxed, talking and just going with the traffic flow.

I did not even see this coming. One car, an old grey Honda Station wagon – I think the driver wanted to change lanes – came flying from the far-right lane. The driver must have done this without even checking the lanes. This car came fast and smashed into my driver's side. It hit the right side headlamp area, breaking the cosmetic rubber seal, stripping it off, and damaging the whole fender, together with the right headlamp casing.

It was super-fast, deafening loud and frightening. Both vehicles came to an immediate halt, debris of the smashed parts scattered on the road. The loud bang on my side door felt like somebody had hit it with a massive sledgehammer.

You couldn't miss that something wrong had just happened. I, nor my passenger, could even give a good narration of how it had happened. It was a typical ambush, a sudden attack, and crash, bang, silent. The only sound was that of the vehicle engine and the music from the car speakers. We both went quiet and numb.

All I can remember is seeing this object flying towards me, and all at once, we were parked side by side in the middle of the highway with the other car stopping at a very rough angle, its left headlamp pinned to my right-side fender. We both came to a dangerous halt, with no time to check for safety regarding the other vehicles flying past us.

With the damaged vehicle parts dangling and scratching the road, this impact was about 200 metres from Hale Road intersection. The other driver started their car and dragged it forward like nothing had happened and kept going till they turned left into Hale Road, then they came to stop about fifty metres off Tonkin Highway. With my damaged Elantra, I managed to start it and drove along following the other car left into Hale Road and came to stop behind it. Then the drama started.

I came out of my vehicle and walked to the other car to talk to the driver. The first tell-tale signs were the state of the vehicle. It was old, filthy, lots of scratch marks and uncared for. The boot and the back seats were roughly packed with dirty unfolded linen, household items and scattered cutlery.

The driver was ready and had lowered her window waiting for me. A driver and a passenger were in the car, two ladies who appeared to be less shaken than I.

"You almost killed me," I said.

"What do you mean?" she replied.

I looked at her for a minute in disbelief, at the same time assessing the vehicle and its two occupants.

"Sorry, mate, I didn't see you," she said, looking towards her passenger who seemed not to care about what was going on or what had just happened.

I chose not to take the option of questioning her further but to exchange details. Quickly she said to me,

"That's not very extensive damage, it should be less than $500.00 to fix, so we don't need to call the police, but just take the details."

At that moment I got into a state of confusion. First, I had a passenger on board, second, my vehicle was damaged, third, I was busy thinking of the consequences of that incident to my financial wellbeing of the day. Now I was face to face with this seemingly aggressive talking woman.

Anyway, with a quick assessment, I told myself that maybe yes, the damage would be less than $500 to fix.

Then I asked for her driver's license.

She announced that she didn't have one. I looked at her with clear amazement. "What's your physical address?" I enquired.

She didn't answer that for a while, then later said that she didn't have a home – she told me she was homeless.

At that point, I realised I was standing on the roadside which was very dangerous with fast traffic flowing past me. I decided to walk right round to the passenger side so that I could speak to her standing on the safer side. As I was walking around, I noticed further damages to her vehicle, which clearly showed a sign of uncaring and rough attitude on her part.

Standing on the passenger side door, I asked again for any other form of identification. She then pulled out a

Medicare card and carelessly handed it over to me. While this was happening, I could see that her passenger, a slim built lady in her mid-twenties I guess, kept giggling and insanely talking to herself. I took a discreet quick but good glance at her and concluded she was drunk. This all happened so quickly I had no time for a clear, fair and straight mind assessment and conclusion. When I look back and replayed the scene, I was very sure both were drunk and probably on drugs.

I grabbed the Medicare card and walked back to my car to write the details down. Then it came to my mind that it was easy for me to take a picture of that size of the card using my mobile phone. Yes, I quickly pulled out my phone and took the pictures. It also quickly came to my mind that I should take pictures of the vehicle number plates and the damaged section of both vehicles. When I finished and walked back to hand over her Medicare card, she climbed out of the vehicle and aggressively approached me.

"I saw you taking pictures of that card. I have details of my kids on it. You can delete that right now!" she barked, taking a threatening stance and coming to my face as close as she could.

Again, I was caught unaware. At the back of my mind, I took it on board that yes, it may have been wrong to take a photo of the card, but I was not sure if she had a valid point that I should not include the details of her kids in the photo. At the same time, it was impossible to take the photo without including the kids because it is one card with a list of names on it. Luckily enough I had taken several photographs of the card, so I deleted only two and remained with the rest.

As I handed back the card, I once again asked for her physical address. I know very well from my previous accident experience that physical address is a requirement with the insurance details.

This time she shouted back, "I told you that I am homeless, and I live in my car. I told you that!!"

"In that case let's call the police," I put to her.

Then she quickly came up with another new story. One that caught me off guard.

"I'm sorry about what just happened. I've given you details on my card. I do not have a home, I live in my car I told you that long back. I'm sorry, I must go because I'm rushing. I have a sick child in the hospital emergency at Armadale Hospital. You know, my dear, no one is hurt here and there is no property damage over $500, I'm sorry I have to go right now."

What would you do? Again, I got twisted. I'm now thinking, what's more important … this woman going to see her child in hospital or me insisting on getting what she said she doesn't have. The two cars are both drivable, just cosmetic damage on my vehicle, on hers, whatever the extent of damage, that was not my problem.

Without saying anything further she started her vehicle and took off. She made a quick U-turn on Hale Road as the traffic was clear and came to a standstill on traffic lights at the intersection with Tonkin Highway.

I'm left standing there with pictures in my phone, no physical address, no police involvement, my passenger looking restless and ready to go. The important thing was that we were safe, only cosmetic damages on the vehicle. Nothing should stop us from proceeding with our trips. I jumped in the vehicle and took off; did a quick U-turn, like she did. There was no danger in doing this as the traffic was still clear and I came to a standstill just behind her car.

We were just quiet in the car with my passenger. Then he said, "You should have called the police; I really suspect those people were on drugs and did not want the police to get involved."

I told him of the pictures I had taken, of the car number plates, the damages, and the Medicare card. Still, I regretted there was no way I could have forced her to give me her physical address details.

The light went green, and we both turned left onto Tonkin Highway southbound. With me right behind her car, I was very keen to follow her and see if she would go towards Armadale Hospital. Sure enough, I was right behind her for a good while. We cruised up Tonkin Highway past Welshpool Road intersection. With the lights green on our side, it was a nice easy flow. Now I noticed her increasing speed. She started zigzagging along the way, changing from lane to lane. We came to stop at the intersection with Kelvin Road, her car about four cars ahead of me in the inner lane.

My passenger and I were now very keen to see where she was going and to keep an eye on her in case anything happened, and we were ready to be witnesses.

We took off after a short while on the intersection and again she sped off, this time again zigzagging from lane to lane speeding up in the process possibly trying to be away from us as much as she could. As there was a fair bit of traffic, and I was maintaining my legal speed limit, she disappeared in the traffic maze. We were left behind speechless.

As we approached the intersection of Mills Road in Gosnells, I saw her vehicle speeding down that road towards inner Gosnells. Straight away I knew I had been outwitted; she was not even going to the hospital – she got away with it. My next move was how to deal with it, and that is the police report and the damaged vehicle.

I drove my passenger to Byford down Tonkin Highway in silence. All I could think about was the regret that I did not call the police at the scene of the accident. Anyway, it was too late to regret over a decision and action already taken.

I dropped my regular passenger at his house in Byford and disconnected the phone app from the Uber platform and went home to park the vehicle.

Luckily, at that time, I had two vehicles registered for Uber duties. The next big task was how to deal with the mess I had been left in by this minor incident.

Now the next thing was to do the insurance claim. I went online straight away and completed the claim; rang my insurance company and notified them of the incident. They insisted I obtain the physical address of the other person. Without delay, I went to the nearest police station with the details of the Medicare Card I had collected from the other driver. I showed the card to the police and told them the details of the Tonkin Highway incident.

All I wanted was for them to access the details of that person using the card number and the vehicle registration I had given them. They immediately declined the request. The reason was that they do not give such information to individuals. Such matters should be done by the insurance, they advised. They had more weight to contact the police with such a request than an individual.

So, I returned home and contacted my insurance again; explained to them that I did not get the physical address of the other person because they said they were homeless. I advised them to use the Medicare Card details I had given them to proceed with the claim. Still they insisted they wanted those details and I was supposed to go and get them before they started the claim process.

We went back and forth for a while, resulting in me making about two trips to the police station. Finally, I decided to write an e-mail to the insurance company. In that email, I explained to them how I had completed a police report online; how I had been to the police in person four times. The fact that I had an accident with someone who was homeless and they didn't have a physical address is not something I could be held responsible for.

Again, they insisted there was no way someone who owns and drives a car can be homeless, even if they live in it.

That was when I realised this (Australian) insurance company subcontracted a Call Centre to a South African company. During all my communications through email and phone calls, I was talking to someone in South Africa. According to them, homeless meant someone with completely nothing. I observed that we were not understanding each other.

This time I rang them again and demanded to talk to the Call Centre Manager. Someone picked up the phone. We spoke briefly, me narrating my story to the attentive call centre staff member. Again, we failed to understand each other. On my persistence to talk to the Manager, the humble staff member decided to do the very old traditional Call centre trick to fix difficult customers. I was put on hold forever.

As determined as I was, I chose to stay put. After an excruciating lengthy period, somebody picked up the phone and enquired about my story again. The whole cycle started all over. I explained my story to this new person over the phone. This time I was put through to the boss.

I told the manager my whole story in detail again. He then opened my file and noticed that I had been in communication with his team on several occasions. I was then asked to put my story in writing, which I did straight after the phone conversation.

In that email, I explained my efforts in taking the details of the accident. My immediate action to make an online police report and going to the police station to try to get the details of the other person, and the police advice on my efforts.

I explained to them the importance of the Australian Medicare card and how important it is as an official document to identify a person. I explained why the police wouldn't deal with me as an individual but would with them as a company and that it was their job to go get the rest of the information. This is the reason we pay for insurance and I was convinced that they were supposed to do such a job.

After about two days I received a phone call advising me that I should take my vehicle to their nominated accident repairer. They had acknowledged my claim. Two weeks later, the vehicle was fixed to perfection, and ready to go at no cost to me.

Yes, finally it was done but this was after putting up a fight with the insurance. From that time on I temporarily took my Elantra off the road, to be used as a private family vehicle only.

The Plain Clothes Police

Be warned: you will never know who you are talking to; who is sitting next to you, or who is sharing a ride with you. If you have nothing to hide like me then feel free to talk to anyone and discover as you go.

That is exactly what happened one night on a ride from Thornlie to the city. One Friday night about 9.00 pm I went to pick up this other fella from a house in a popular southern suburb of Perth.

I arrived at this nice, average suburban house. Neat and well fenced, gated, nice manicured lawns out the front, perfectly sealed driveway sliding past tall trees into the perfect courtyard well illuminated by strategically positioned solar lamp posts.

Without much delay, I saw a gentleman coming out of the house carrying some items, with both hands neatly and tightly bound on his chest. A tall man, he must have been in his late twenties, he was well built, strong and muscular. Clad in Brooklyn straight jeans, tight-fitting short-sleeved indigo dye shirt and an assortment of glittering accessories. His looks and appearance gave me the impression of an ordinary, everyday young Australian man out for a weekend night drink.

I unlocked the vehicle and he clambered in. Just as he made himself comfortable, I checked that he was the right person. We both agreed and I took off. He really looked and was a typical easy-going fella. He started by politely asking if it was okay with me for him to bring his drinks into the car.

The obvious answer is always yes on such requests. I am always blown away by such humble people. I love such courtesy and politeness. A clear sign of regard and appreciation of another person, even though he knew the answer would be nothing but yes.

I assured him to feel free. A short while into a short talk, he went on to ask me how the job was, of course meaning my driving job.

I told him that so far, the night was going well – there had been no funny incidences and I was looking forward to a night with no skirmishes. To prolong the discussion, I went on to give a narration of how things can quickly go wrong in this type of job; how I can end up with nasty people who can spoil the night in an instant. I also assured him that not all people were nasty. I told him that there were a whole lot of nice people out there as well. The only problem was that you didn't know who, it was always guesswork, it was just taking chances, that anything could go wrong at any time.

Then, I concluded by saying, "I don't know what goes on in the minds of the police officers, considering all the people and cases they deal with. Imagine all the cases they get involved with in their daily tasks."

He cast a glance at me, flashed a smile accompanied by a soft laugh, and quietly said to me, "What do you think?"

I told him I thought being in the police frontline duties and dealing with the public every day one would end up not very sociable but very suspicious in their interaction with everyone. I thought it was a type of job that would make you very unfriendly and always keeping a distance from anyone.

I said, "It will be good if some police officer writes out a document for a one-year Journal of their daily duties and encounters. I'm sure it will be a best-seller, as everybody would be keen to read all about it."

"Yes, you are right," he said.

He kept his cool for a while like he was thinking over something. This was something I recalled later but as it was happening, I didn't pick it up. After a short while he went on to ask me if I had ever driven strange people in my daily duties, like suspicious persons or anyone you think might have been up to no good. I, for some reason, told him that most people who use this type of transport are very responsible and don't usually have strange behaviours.

He nodded quietly then slid his right hand into his side trouser pocket. Slowly he pulled out something and flashed it at me.

Oops! that was his identification. My rider was a police officer! It was a neatly printed card with clearly visible white and blue strips on a blue binding neck ribbon with metal clippings at the point of contact of the card and the ribbon.

Yes, surprise, surprise! He was one of our guys in blue, an off-duty Australian police officer. He later explained to me that he was an officer from Kalgoorlie, and as he flashed the card to me, I could see the distinct national emblem, portrait photo, and name, convincing me that he was indeed a police officer.

He briefly told me that he'd been deployed to Kalgoorlie after graduation from the Police Academy and he was in

Perth because that's his hometown and he'd come for a friend's birthday function that very weekend.

As he was explaining this to me, I was busy thinking about how things could quickly go wrong if you were up to no good. I would have been in trouble quick if I was doing something illegal. Right in my car, besides me was an undercover police officer. How good it is to be straight and to do right all the time and to be careful with anyone we meet, as you will never know who is who until you know them. Do not judge people, you will never know, and be careful and vigilant when meeting people you don't know!

The Free Long Ride

One Monday afternoon, I was in the northern suburbs, a typical first day of the week. You expect it to be quiet, but you are there if a ride comes along, which will bring great excitement. In the city along Fitzgerald Street, I received a request.

On arrival at the pickup point, I saw this young man, my guess, in his twenties. Of medium height, slim build, unkempt beard, he was dressed in faded Austin skinny jeans, a jumper, and canvas sneakers, and an oversized green jumper-shirt with a distinct Nike "Just Do It" motif. An Australian bush hat sat on his small round head.

The long carrying strap of a brown leather bag draped across his chest, the bag hanging on the side of his left hip. His self-presentation gave the portrait of a young musician or artist. He opened the door and confirmed his identity and that he was going to Rockingham, a good distance – about 46 kilometres which, according to Google map calculations, would take forty-two minutes.

A nice long drive, I thought. It was going to be *very* good drive for a not-so-busy Monday afternoon. Instantly the fella jumps in and we took off straight away. I did a quick U-turn and drove up Fitzgerald Street towards the city; turned right into Newcastle Street, less than a kilometre up towards Leederville then a sharp left to hook up into

Kwinana Freeway. We blended into the fast and easy-going traffic heading south. With the music booming in the car, and nothing much to talk about, my passenger eased himself into a smooth sleep in the back seat. We cruised down this southern freeway and exited the freeway into Thomas Road. With the GPS in perfect working order, I negotiated the streets and bends and was at his destination in exactly forty-three minutes.

My passenger had woken up about fifteen minutes before the end of the trip. All along the way, he had not said a word. Now as we approached the driveway, he said, "Ahh! change of plans. I have to go back to the city, just wait for me here. I want to quickly get in the house and will be out in a flash."

Sure, enough he got out and disappeared into the house. I liked that sudden change of plans. That was going to be an advantage to me, a guaranteed drive back to the city with someone in the car. When doing such a job it is always an advantage to have a return trip with someone on board.

Instead of ending the trip, he just changed to a new destination address.

In a short time, the guy came out of the house, jumped into the car and we started our city-bound journey. I got myself in a mindset ready to tackle the forty-two-kilometre return trip. With an assortment of Rap music, my rider kept himself busy by singing along with the songs, just a happy looking fella this time.

As we were driving along, I noticed a few mood changes with him. One time he could be singing at a very high-pitched voice then the next moment he goes very low like he doesn't know the song. On two occasions he asked me where we were, and how far we were from the city. For someone who lived in that suburb and travelled up and down that road every day, one wouldn't expect a question like that.

With the music and mood changes and a series of disjointed questions and lines of discussions, we finally arrived in the city. This time he directed me to go to East Perth. We went to some old building which looked like an old printing house, with lots of rubbish and papers all over the back of the building right where we parked.

He directed me to drive into an alleyway. I did and parked the Elantra just behind a broken gate tied together with rusty wires. Just like he did in Rockingham, again he instructed me to wait and he walked and disappeared into the building through the back door. People were walking up and down in the building but I could not figure out exactly what was happening or what type of business it was as there was no sign-writing on it, just a blank old brick building.

Two young girls and a middle-aged man walked out of that building through the same door. They walked into a corner next to some overfilled rubbish bins and started smoking on that filthy spot.

I remained calm waiting for my client to come out. For some reason, everything didn't look right. My conclusion was that maybe it must be these upcoming modern-day Tech and digital companies with these young executives as is the current world trend.

After about ten minutes my rider emerged, strolled straight to and climbed into the car; he gave a new wave of instructions.

"Ah! again change of ideas – let's go back to Rockingham."

At this point, I was no longer in the best mood to deliver

that service. Uber rides are normally ten to twenty minutes. This forty-two-minute ride to and from Rockingham was a bit exhausting. This is not the intention of such a business to have someone in the car for that long. Yes, it would be good business but very tiresome. It was not supposed to be like that. It would be best if you go for such a long journey to drop the person, then somebody else pick them up on the return trip and that is how it should be.

Instead of questioning, I decided to do the right thing, which was just to change the destination address back to the Rockingham address, and that's what I did.

Again, I started driving and negotiating my way out of the city from East Perth through Wellington Street and onto the Kwinana Freeway. This time my rider was quiet and kept fidgeting with some papers in his little carry bag. I kept a constant observation of his behaviour as I drove. Traffic was a bit heavy this time and the road speed was greatly compromised.

From the back seat, my passenger again fell into a snooze, he just went fast asleep flat, just like that. All the way to Rockingham it was just me in the car and the radio music providing entertainment as I cruised southwards on the freeway.

If I had been on my own from the time I picked this guy up to that moment, I would have gone for a break but that never happened. Driving can become a burden in such instances. Now everything appeared hard and less enjoyable. All I wanted this time was to get to his destination and get him out of my car and for me to breathe a sigh of relief.

The landmark features along the freeway made life easy for me. I was now tired but this time I looked forward to reaching a landmark feature. Joining the freeway from the city, the next feature for me was the Narrows Bridge. Driving over that bridge gives a good view of the river on both sides and a difference in mood from the noise of fast-flowing traffic.

From there I look forward to being cautious on the South Perth off-ramp. This section of the road has a lower speed limit and you must be cautious as other vehicles are changing lanes to get into the South Perth off-ramp. A smooth drive past this section of the road, get you in this big mood as the speed limit changes to 100 km/hr. Vehicles are speeding and you have to keep the pace, and at the same time enjoy the new scenery of an array of beautiful buildings and apartment hotels and gardens overlooking the South Perth offshore.

On the southside, the river flows far to the horizon, a spectacle you can just enjoy as you concentrate on the road ahead. This will immediately lead you past Canning Bridge Station seeing some cars taking the off-ramp and say goodbye to that section of the road. Then there is a need to look for the cars merging from Canning Highway into the freeway. With the high speed and the oncoming Mt Henry Bridge section, the concentration is high again. This time you approach the bridge overlooking the boats scattered on the river below and the beautiful scenery of the suburbs overlooking that section of the river. It is a short distance of scenic view and there is not much time to enjoy the spectacle below because of the need to concentrate much more on the road. Any mishap on this section of the road will be a major disaster and delay the traffic flow. Hence every driver needs to be very careful. A cruise past the bridge shows you the road signs of the major incoming roads South Road and Leach Highway.

By that point you have the feel of the flow and the driving is now in your blood and you are really refocused on your driving. It's a point of no return.

I kept focused and enjoying my drive, even though a bit worried about this unusual movement. Yes, it's business, but this time I was acting like this guy's day chauffeur.

With traffic going smooth and no incidents on the way, it was a nice and easy drive. Going past Fiona Stanley Hospital, I went into automatic mode and just focused on my long drive to the Thomas Road off-ramp. I didn't take much notice of other places and landmarks anymore. The next thing I knew I was negotiating the streets of Rockingham with the GPS leading me to the place we'd been an hour ago.

We arrived back at the house and my rider was up again. This time I expected him to say, "Thank you for the ride and go well."

This did not happen. Just like last time, he again instructed, "Wait here," and disappeared into the house.

So once more I was left waiting and the account still running and waiting for his instructions to end the trip. Meanwhile, I was thinking to myself and wishing him not to come and tell me that the trip was to continue. All I wanted now was to drop him off and I go, but customer service ethics tells you the "the customer is king." So, I had to stay put and wait for the King to come out with fresh instructions.

A few minutes later he came out of the house this time dressed differently, that little brown strip bag left behind. He now wore a black leather jacket, and a near-new pair of running shoes and a silver wristwatch gleaming out from the far end of his right-hand leather jacket arm. It looked like he had gone into the house for a quick refreshment and a change of clothes.

He came to my driver's side door and asked me how much it was for the duration he had been with me in the car. I was happy that he was also aware that we were doing something unusual. Unfortunately, I did not have access to his balance amount. This was something you can only access after you have closed the account, and it takes a few minutes to calculate and show the balance.

In the rich and famous style, he said to me, "Change of plans again, buddy, let's go back to the city."

Yes, I agreed. In customer service, the motto is "Your wish is my command."

That was the way to go, but to be honest, not on that day and at that hour. I was now really exhausted and disliked the request/instruction. The fact that we'd been together that long was too much to bear. Then, on second thought, in focus with these instructions, it was going to be to my advantage to go back to the city with him on board again. Such a location on a mid-week afternoon, it was not common to get such a long ride. The consequences would be to drive forty-two kilometres back to the city with no one on board. In such a small business, that is a big loss.

Without questioning him as he made himself comfortable in the back seat, I took off and headed my way back to the city. The best thing to do was to set my mind up for the endurance of the long drive ahead.

I forecast my driving to the destination, a second forty-two-kilometre return trip. Since I had driven this trip up and down a few times, I was now in the automatic mode and found it easy to negotiate my trip around the bends and on straight roads leading to the freeway. This time I did not take much notice of the landmarks on my way. They were just there, fixed and usual. The drive-up Rockingham

Road, and the zoom past the Kwinana industrial area, was very swift with little heavy traffic. In no time I was soon turning right into Thomas Road. The long stretch of 80 km/hr witnessed me cruising past Kwinana Dirt Bike Ride area and bushlands on the north and the build-up Kwinana residential area on the south side of Thomas Road. That stretch gave me a beautiful and smooth drive and easy traffic flow that led into an easy diverging slide and merge into Kwinana freeway northbound.

This part of the freeway has always been a notorious stretch. Traffic for some reason slows down and causes a build-up with traffic merging from Anketell, Rowley and Gibbs Roads.

Just like the other few trips, we had up and down that freeway, we were quiet. Just the radio sound in the background and this time my rider was engaged on the phone. We had been together for too long. I was tired of talking about anything. Even the effort of coming up with small talk, joke or a question was now out of me.

As we approached Armadale Road, at a build-up speed of about 80 km an hour, my phone popped up a message. A direct message from the Uber command centre.

It read: "Drop that person immediately!"

Immediately the passenger's details disappeared from my phone – it went clear into a new rider receiving mode. When that happens you know you are ready to receive other calls. My predicament at that moment was that I had this guy with me in the car, and in the middle of the freeway with slow-moving heavy traffic. It was a moment of quick decision, something had to be done, and quick. Drop him there or negotiate to keep going and pay at the end or stop the car and make him reorder before we can proceed with the trip.

I decided to deliver the bad news. I explained to him what had just happened and that we could not continue with the trip because he was no longer officially my customer. The system had erased him.

He then tried to make another booking, but the system rejected him. He tried to call somebody and that somebody gave a lengthy explanation over the phone. In the end, the phone conversation abruptly ended.

Now the next move was to get him out of my vehicle, but that was going to be inconsiderate because we were in the middle of the freeway. So I decided to let him know that we would keep driving towards the original destination, and I would drop him immediately on the first legal stop point in the city. Deal sealed, we headed on with our trip.

There was an intense atmosphere in the vehicle as we both knew our situation. I was not supposed to have that person enjoying a free ride, that was a ride with no documentation and a good risk on me. If that person had decided to attack me, there were no justifiable or supporting reasons why he was still taking a ride when his name was wiped off the official register. Same as if there was an accident, I was equally going to be in trouble for giving somebody a free ride.

At the back of the vehicle in the passenger seat, the guy was shaking his head and swearing about the disconnection and some other problems with him he muttered about.

Not long from there, we were right in the city, the swishing noise of vehicles leaving the city in the peak hour traffic was loud and ongoing. I veered towards the Mounts Bay Road off-ramp and came to a stop on the first available spot along Mounts Bay Road eastbound.

That marked the end of our trip, and I instructed him to leave, regardless of where he wished to go. That was as far as I could safely drop him.

I had a combination of a sigh of relief, and a regret that I spoiled my day's potential earnings moving around with this guy up and down to Rockingham and I was likely not to be paid for that.

Immediately I rang Uber Office and explained to them what had happened in the day. The person on the other end of the line looked for the details of that rider, and they regretted to tell me that the rider was not a very good customer. His account had been put on hold.

I will leave it to you to imagine my disappointment, and there is nothing you can do about it. That is the essence of the service industry, such things happen. In any case, there is always an assurance that good will always come. Such incidences are rare and should not be a source of discouragement.

Maccas Chicken Nuggets

Early one morning, around 4.00 am, I was in the streets of Mosman Park dropping a passenger I had picked from Perth International Airport. At such an early hour ride calls are unusual. By chance, you may get one going *to* the airport, especially the Fly-in-Fly-out people, but that area does not have many Fly-in-Fly-out workers. With that in mind, I decided to go to Fremantle which is more of a mixed-up place and anything can happen anytime, and anyone can be going anywhere any hour.

I accelerated my Hyundai Elantra towards Fremantle, meandering the inner roads and merging into Stirling Highway. With not much traffic flowing, it did not take me long to reach the heart of Fremantle. As I slowly moved around looking for a nice spot to park and wait for calls to come, I received one and headed straight to the pick-up location. It was easy for me as I had been to that place several times.

The streets were empty, and rubbish lay all over the pavements. Groups of people sat scattered around the outside restaurant tables. Cleaners were already coming to do their jobs. The mobile street cleaning mini-utility trucks were busy preparing the place for the next business day. It is quite exciting to observe how they clean these streets when the pubs are closed, ensuring an early morning immaculate presentation. The window cleaners, the road street cleaning vehicles with big round wire brushes make a loud noise when they are revolving, rubbing and scrubbing the street and sucking all the rubbish and dust strewn everywhere. The flashing security lights on the trucks and the dimness of the streets and alleyways gives a serious business day preparation mood.

The homeless people, fully covered in rugged clothes and tucked in sharp street corners, the abandoned shopping trolleys and the general messiness of the place after the evening's hype and gigs, all created a busy morning for the cleaners.

I meandered my way to the exact pickup point. As I arrived, I saw a group of people, a middle-aged male and female sitting around a street-fixed, wooden restaurant table. I guessed them to be my clients and waited.

In no time I saw a Caucasian man of medium height, strong build, and neat and well-trimmed hair, in his late twenties, staggering out of an alleyway. The streetlight reflected well on him showing his brown bomber jacket, a Commons shirt, and well-fitting Phoenix blue slim jeans. All matched up with his Kingstone Chelsea leather boots. Perfect attire for the night, I thought. He stood about two metres from the group. In a slurred and less commanding voice, he invited them to get into the car with him. Two sitting at the front shook their heads, and the rest kept looking down at the table. He stood there, felt his pockets, looked left and right and then grabbed the car door and slid in.

I checked and confirmed his name and we both agreed. Strapping his seat belt on, but finding it difficult to relax, he quietly said, "Let's shoot off," and I shifted the car into Drive, and we zoomed out of that place.

A very jovial and friendly man who, without much delay,

announced that he wanted a kebab. Just as we took off, we just struck a chord of like minds. Even though slightly under the influence, he was that type of person who was easy going and generous with his jokes. In a very high-pitched, friendly voice he said: "I said kebabs, my brother from another mother!!"

Pushing his car seat back and dropping both hands he then went to sleep.

To make life easy I stopped and consulted Google. There were no more kebab shops open at that hour of the day. Since his destination was Kardinya and we were going to travel up Leach Highway from Fremantle I decided to stop over at McDonald's in Melville. I asked him, and he agreed in his half-sleep state. Then he insisted that he buy me chicken nuggets as well. I declined as I noticed that, in his near drunken state, it might look like I had taken advantage of his inebriation, so I told him a good straight "No, thank you."

I drove my vehicle out of the quiet Fremantle maze, up along South Terrace and left into Norfolk Street. I approached the roundabout and continued into Parry Street. At this point, Fremantle starts to ease out and the streets become less of a maze. About 200 metres up at the traffic lights, I turned right into High Street and from there it was a nice straight drive to my destination as that stretch of road leads into Leach Highway. In no time I was well past Carrington Road and up the hill. I could see Melville showing up. I cruised down Leach Highway and past Melville Motors on the left-hand side and came to a halt at the intersection of Leach Highway and Lakes Road.

After a short stop, we veered off Leach Highway on to the shopping centre and into the well-lit and signposted Macca's outlet. Now this guy asks me again if I wanted some chicken nuggets. With his state of mind, again I declined the offer.

There is a problem with such offers: one can wake up the next morning and deny that they offered to buy you. Then, in the end, it would appear that I took advantage of his drunken impaired judgment.

From there he goes on to insist that he will buy me something to nibble on.

Carefully I steered the vehicle to the ordering points in one of the drive-through lanes.

This time he was sitting up straight and cleared his throat ready to place the order. When the attendant's voice crackled through the speakers, asking us to place the order, he went on to say, "One Quarter pounder meal and a frozen coke," and after a short pause added, "and six chicken nuggets, no drink."

I noticed that he hadn't suggested any sauces to go with the chicken nuggets, and did not want to remind him, just in case he had a plan. In the meantime, the attendant asked if he needed anything else, and he confirmed that the order was complete.

I slid the gear lever into Drive and we crawled forward to the payment window, then on to the food pickup point.

As he had requested that he wanted a bite earlier on in the trip, it looked like he was really looking forward to his food. He instructed me to park the Elantra on a spot off the Maccas drive-through. With his supposedly dirty and obviously unwashed hands – whoever knows where they'd been or what they'd touched – he opened the chicken nuggets.

By then the aroma of the food was all over the vehicle making my taste buds go watery and forcing my lips into an involuntary licking action. He put his hands into the nugget box and lifted three of them.

With a genuine sign of hospitality, he says, "Yes, my good friend, you can have these. Let's munch, my mate!!"

I was left with no room to decide but just to thank him for his offer and accepted the three nuggets. Now you can imagine this, I'm now left with three nuggets on my left hand, no serviette, no sauce, regardless of the hygiene practice of that moment, I had to munch them.

Picture this: I just picked up this guy from the closing pub. He just walked into the car. I don't know what he was doing in the pub, what those hands were touching or anything else he's done with his hands. Then this guy right now is saving me these three nuggets with his bare and uncleaned hands. Just like that, chicken nuggets, no sauce, three of them.

There is nothing wrong with eating food or being given food anytime but it remains a fact that food is nicer when it is served covered, and handed in a more acceptable way – some standard of hygiene practice in place. None of these were there in this offer. Naturally, that renders the food unpalatable, so was my case at that moment.

Now my dilemma was what to do with the nuggets. The guy was opening his quarter pounder, and surely was looking forward to seeing me eating the nuggets as well.

I did put them in the cup holder between the front seats and started the vehicle, shooting off from our parking spot to the destination.

"Eat them," he encourages me.

At that point, I was left with no excuse. I gnawed one of them with difficulty just to make him happy and be seen to be appreciating the offer. I just did not like them. The taste was terrible, dry without sauce and the combination of my perception, it was just off-putting. It is true that food tastes better when both visual and presentation are tempting.

We meandered through the streets of Murdoch with my man enjoying his burger, me struggling to eat the unpalatable three chicken nuggets. When we finally arrived at his destination, he thanked me for the ride and again asked if I enjoyed the nuggets.

Of course, I was in a corner. I had to fake it that they were delicious. He climbed out of the car and we parted ways, leaving me behind with the nasty after-taste in my mouth from the unpleasant experience of the consumption of the nuggets served with dirty hands, and dry with no sauce.

The Brazilian Bush Party

After dropping some guys off from a Northbridge night out, I decided to stay in Scarborough Beach.

The digital clock on my car dashboard reflected one and a half hours past midnight. Instead of driving back to the city with high chances of pickups, I decided to stay put in my current location. The early morning sea-breeze chill forced me to leave my engine running and the warm air-con on.

In about five minutes I received a call, and it showed that it was from a house in that very street. There was no point switching on the GPS as the pickup point was about a hundred metres ahead of where I was parked. Without putting the car in full throttle, I crawled along and arrived at this house and saw two young ladies dressed for the night and ready to go.

I unlocked the doors and the two came in. Following the usual procedures, I asked their names to confirm the identity of the caller, all matched up and we shot off. Sliding the trip start button and setting the GPS, I noticed the destination was in Fremantle.

That was an easy nice long drive sliding along West Coast Drive. From our greetings and their back-seat chat, I placed their accents to be from South America, which I later realised was a good guess.

We drove past the western suburb of Cottesloe enjoying the long drive with the sea on one side – nice and quiet with no traffic. We then filtered into Stirling Highway heading towards Fremantle. Meanwhile, the two girls were busy chatting in the back, and I was enjoying listening to riders' conversations made up of a mixture of English and their Brazilian language.

We went past North Fremantle going across the bridge and filtered into Canning Highway. The route proceeded past the Fremantle city and zoomed across and out heading towards Rockingham.

As we shot out of the city into the western residential areas just before Coogee Beach, the GPS lost its track; showed that the destination was right out in the sea. Having driven past that area many times and, having seen high-rise residential construction taking place and the changing face of the landscape, I thought it might be a tracking error. This is common in most new developments: GPS readings take some time to be uploaded to be able to navigate on the newly built-up areas. So, I thought that was the case with this GPS tracking error that night.

At this point, my passengers noticed my slow driving and realised the GPS error. They were also not very sure of the exact location of the place they were going. All they knew was the place was somewhere around that area. If you look at the area on a physical map, you will see there are new houses and the rest is bushland stretching out and joining the foreshore.

The road network in that area does not clearly show. It shows a network of footpaths zigzagging in the bush and then filtering into the sea. We drove around for a while, going around in circles.

Then we agreed to follow one road which led us into the

bush driving away from the residential area. I took a chance but was not very keen to drive into such thicket in that hour of the day. After a short drive penetrating the bush, I stopped and did a U-turn and headed back to our safe starting point in the residential area.

This time, while we were driving back, we saw another dirt road disappearing again into the bush leading to the beach. I decided to take chance and followed that road. Again, it just meandered in the bush. I felt unsafe and again we made a U-turn and drove back the starting point.

Now, this time the girls decided to ring the person who'd invited them to this party. After a few attempts, the phone was finally picked, and a male voice boomed on the other end.

The caller told them of our current location and was given directions to get to the place. It turned out that the first road we'd abandoned was the right one.

We finally drove into the middle of the bushes, this time with high confidence and certainty of our destination. We drove away from the residential area towards the sea disappearing into the thick and dense bush as the residential area vanished behind us.

Then we heard loud music coming from the bush area and the girls flared up with excitement. I also felt relieved to be safe and certain there was nothing sinister about the bizarre destination, and that we had finally found the place.

They shook their bodies, dancing with the rhythm of the music booming from the speakers outside, at the same time clicking their thumbs and ring fingers to complement the beat. A clear display of ecstasy.

This was it, beachside all-night fun extending into the early hours of the new day. People of various shapes, sizes, and ages dancing, eating and drinking by the beach nowhere near the residential area. Most males had their shirts off, ladies in a hodgepodge of bikinis, tight jeans and wrap-overs of all types. Just an all-night beachfront party in session. You had to be there to see it to believe it.

I was observing this and admitting that I'd never seen such a scene before. Normally this is the time most clubs are closing, and people are heading home, but these party-goers were full-on, not in the mood to go anywhere soon.

Then one of my lady passengers told me, "They don't do this thing here in Australia – this is what we do in Brazil."

Smiling and waving me goodbye, they left the vehicle to join the party, one of them saying, "That's my Brazil, look at that!!"

I drove along the parking area looking for the best place to make a U-turn, all the while enjoying the scene in progress right in front of me. Brazilian all-night beachfront fun on the fringes of Fremantle. It was just a fun atmosphere, far from the maddening crowd. Everybody looked happy and were enjoying themselves, no supervision, just a group that must have organised themselves to have a good time in the middle of the night.

What an observation and experience, something I've never been involved in or seen before. Brilliant, I said to myself as I negotiated my vehicle out of the party scene car park and back to my driving thing.

The Byford Country Club

It was about 10.30 pm and I was at home in Byford. I planned to head towards the airport. As I was getting out of the house a call came through. I glanced at the screen and realised it was a local call. The location was familiar so I did not need to use the GPS to navigate to the pickup spot.

As I drew closer, I switched on the GPS. The location was at the intersection of Thomas Road and South Western Highway. From my knowledge of this place, I know of no houses that face that intersection. I stopped and looked around, expecting to see someone standing somewhere in that area.

With the coming of Uber, these days it is common to pick up people at any location as they use real-time location on GPS, and it is easy to get where they are. On that site is a little dense bush and the Byford town centre noticeboard and sculptures. Nothing else.

I looked around to make sure there was no one then rang, thinking the rider might be somewhere in the bush or in the yard of any of the adjustment 5-acre properties around that area. The call was picked up and the rider told me they were at the Byford Country Club.

I know that area well too and my car was facing the wrong direction. All I had to do was drive less than a kilometre from the intersection and shoot off into Stanley

Avenue, right at the corner of Byford Baptist Church on the right and proceed up towards the hill. I came to the T junction with Linton Street and made a sharp right. A few metres up that road is a clear sight of the Country Club. The recently newly-built Country Club has a nicely built road stretching from Linton Street to this well-designed spacious car park.

Right in the middle of the car park, I saw my riders waiting for me. By their anxious looks, I could tell they were my riders. I halted close to them and instantly they got in. I confirmed the rider's identity: all was good – they were my right people.

The combination suggested to me they were two couples. I did not ask, but from the looks of it, I guessed it must have been the older couple with their son and girlfriend or daughter and boyfriend.

Now the fun began. As we took off, I tried to bring up small talk by letting them know how I stopped at the wrong place when the GPS indicated they were at the intersection of Thomas Road and South Western Highway.

I expected a bit of laughter about that and an appreciation of my efforts to ring them and to navigate to the Country Club when the GPS had failed to pinpoint their exact location.

The younger man just giggled, and said in a sarcastic tone, "Really, how did that happen?"

When I tried to jovially explain the common GPS error, especially when the riders are not careful when they are placing their orders, I had this sudden interjection from the older man.

"Why did you go there? We never put that address. We were just outside the Country Club and that is where we expected you to come and pick us up, and not even to ring us!" His voice boomed, and I could tell from his tone he was highly agitated. This caught me unaware and I did not have an immediate answer to that. The hostility in his voice made me guess that he did not know much about common errors with the GPS.

I quickly concluded this was not the right platform for me to explain to him what had happened. I noticed that after his agitated statement there was an uneasy atmosphere in the car. His fellow passengers felt bad about it. No one had anything to say as a cover-up about it, there was just dead silence in the car.

The older woman decided to come up with a story just to kill the silence. I could tell she was putting in an effort to push away the awkward confrontation. I decided to remain quiet all the way though. Lucky enough, it was only a fifteen-minute drive to their drop off point.

I dropped them at their house in Armadale and the ladies and the younger man said their thanks for the drive and waved goodnight. The older man just crawled out of the car and sauntered away without saying anything.

I continued driving, telling myself that sometimes silence is the best medicine.

What could have happened if I had tried to explain or answer back in a similar pitched voice?

The Rider Drives

Early Thursday morning, around 4.00 am, I dropped a passenger in Armadale. I'd had a long and busy night and had been driving nonstop throughout the night. As Armadale is near my home, a little thought kept telling me it was time to go home and sleep.

Just as I was contemplating that thought, I received a call from Byford. I saw the address and I knew the road well, so I pointed my Elantra to Byford and headed towards Tourmaline Boulevarde for my waiting rider. From my current location, there was no point switching on the navigation as I could easily navigate my way to the pickup point.

From experience, I know very well that high chances are calls at such times are likely to be going to the airport from FIFO workers. So, as I was driving to this point I lowered my windows to allow a maximum flow of fresh air to keep me fresh and awake.

At the back of my mind, I was hesitant to take the long thirty-five-minute drive from Byford to the airport.

In no time, while too immersed in the thoughts of the long drive, I was already parking in the driveway of my pickup point.

The lights went on in the house and I knew they were ready to go. In no time the front door opened, and a male came out and walked to the car, a seemingly easy-going guy with a happy looking face. That was always a good start when people came in such a mood, you looked forward to a pleasant drive. I opened the boot for him to place his carry luggage and he came to the front seat. Instead of just opening the door, getting in, sitting down and strapping on his seat belt, he jovially greeted me.

"Can I come in?" he said, opening the door and standing outside waiting for me to respond.

Already ignited into a pleasant mood I said, "Yes please, come in. I'm here at your service."

He smiled and came in but took his time to close the door. Strapping the seat belt on, he said to me, "You have been driving for the whole night, have you?"

"That's correct," I responded, not even trying to guess where that line of conversation was heading to.

As though he knew what I was thinking when I was driving to pick him up, he added, "If you have been driving the whole night you must be tired by now?"

I truthfully told him that I started driving from midnight and the time was now 4:30 am. This means that I had a total of four and a half hours behind the wheel. So, I told him that I cannot declare myself very tired. I opted for that kind of answer as I was not sure of his intentions with such a question.

Then he said, "I'm more than happy to give you a hand, brother."

"What do you mean?" I queried.

"I'm more than happy to drive for you from here to the airport, and that will give you a short rest. It's up to you … I'm just offering." He gave a little laugh and smiled.

From my observation and judgment, I had no doubt this offer was genuine and I found no reasonable grounds to object to that.

"My pleasure," I replied. "I assume you have your driver's licence with you right now?" I threw in the friendly question.

I took off my seat belt and walked out and round to the passenger side, as he did the same, coming to the driver's side.

Confidently he checked the controls of the vehicle, adjusted his seat, and strapped on the belt, and we took off.

"It is good. I will drive for now. For this time relax and stretch out a little, that will pump a bit of energy in you when I get off," he said.

Such offers and gestures are not usual. I accepted his offer and allowed him to drive my vehicle with no reservations; did not see anything dubious about it. I just saw a case of liking each other in an instant, or someone who knows a bit about the driving I was doing and just wanted to give me some relief.

I took the passenger's seat with ease and saw us cruising up Tonkin Highway during early morning light traffic. I did not initiate any short stories throughout the trip, the fella was also not keen to talk but you can tell that it was just genuine silence. He concentrated on his driving and I took my offered rest.

How good it feels to be driven by someone else who appears very confident and very cautious driving. In about thirty-five minutes we were driving past the airport spaghetti junctions. Past the triple roundabout at the domestic airports and we were in the queue on the departure point. As he was parking the vehicle, he said, "There you go, my good friend … how was my driving?"

"Excellent," I said as he parked the vehicle and undid his seatbelt and climbed out to get his bags from the back.

"Thanks for the help," I said as we shook hands and he reminded me to drive safely.

I took to the road and drove off amazed at such a little act of thoughtfulness. How some people can make your day shine by throwing in such surprises. For me, that was a great seal of kindness. That moment gave me a moment of relief as driving is tiresome. That rest, while I still charged him for the trip, was mind-blowing and a challenge to pass on that benevolence to someone else someday.

Oops!! Wrong crowd

On this day I planned to drive from 5.00 pm to midnight. This was because I had a plan the next day and could not do my usual early morning drive. I picked up one middle-aged lady from Thornlie going to Kelmscott.

There she was, a clumsy-looking, bulky female clad in an awkward fitting denim mini skirt, very loose Supima tee shirt and an oversized utility green jacket on top. All was complemented by a worn-out of pair Parague sneakers and a Lily Loves wide strap camera bag hanging from her right shoulder.

She came along to the car carrying a plastic carry bag and a cake in a well decorated and fancy, transparent food container. I checked and confirmed her name when she opened the door and asked to put her hand-held items in the back seat. With all the loving care and accuracy, she placed the items down neatly.

"This is a very special day," she said.

Shaking her head and making herself comfortable in the passenger seat, she promised to be a nonstop storyteller. We quickly connected and instantly developed this quick natural liking of each other. You know those moments where you meet someone, and you just keep talking and laughing and you just like each other and a friendly atmosphere is naturally created.

Each side equally participated in the small talk. She

threw up a joke about the special day and what she'd do to anyone who destroyed that cake or anyone who rang her to tell her the event was cancelled. It was just a fun talk, and she was so happy and looking forward to meeting some of her mates at the function. She also thanked Uber for being there any time and that she was going to have a few drinks and it was going to be our responsibility to bring her back home safe. Again, we laughed about that. I then assured her that I may not be nearby to bring her back home; regardless, if not, there would be an Uber vehicle nearby to pick her up and take her back home. I assured her that Uber was always there to save people like her, any time.

"That's what we do," I promised.

Our trip from Thornlie was along Spencer Road which then changes to Corfield Street cutting through Gosnells. As a nice straight drive without much traffic, in no time we were going under the Tonkin Highway underpass, and the road changed name again to Railway Avenue which heralded the announcement of our official entry into the suburb of Kelmscott.

Still during the fun and chatting, I drove for a few more kilometres. We went past a few sharp turns, one or two roundabouts and then a winding curve to a T junction, then a right turn into a cul-de-sac with houses on big yards.

As we approached the end of the road, we saw this other house with the outside front-yard full of people and cars tightly parked along the street. I looked ahead and noticed it was going to be hard for me to go past and look for a perfect parking spot to drop my rider, and then make U-turn to drive away. My rider assessing the congestion of both people and cars and suggested that I stop right there, drop her off, and she could walk to the house. I agreed to that suggestion as it was going to be easier for me. I stopped, and she climbed out, picked up her plastic bag and cake, and we said our farewells. I noticed her confidently walking and disappearing into the crowd. I made a U-turn and drove away.

Less than a kilometre from where I had dropped my rider, I decided to look for a place to park my Elantra and wait for other calls to come. In about five to ten minutes, my phone flashed, signalling the arrival of a new rider call. I looked at the name and instantly recognised it.

It was from the nearby same street where I'd just dropped that last lady rider. Just before I started driving to this pick-up spot a message came along.

It read: Please pick me up again at the same spot that you dropped me a short while ago.

I started driving to that very spot.

Right in front of me was that same lady rider walking out of the crowd coming towards my car. Holding her previously-joked-about *precious* parcel, she looked disheartened, very opposite of her previous jovial mood. Instantly I knew something was not right. I didn't want to throw in any practical joke as I sensed this was not the right time.

She opened the door, sneaked in and awkwardly threw herself down on the passenger seat. Just before I started the trip, I waited a while to give her time to gain her composure. With her eyes fixed on the car rubber floor mat, she told me in a very low and sorrowful voice that she had walked into a funeral session.

"I went to the wrong house – there is a funeral at that house. I got the address wrong, it's so embarrassing."

She'd gone to this house by mistake. When I dropped her, we saw lots of people at that house in the street and took it for granted it was the correct drop-off address. The crowd overflowing into the street gave us the impression it was a party. She had instructed me to drop her as she was equally convinced that it was her correct destination.

She'd walked into that place and realised she was the only Caucasian amongst a crowd of people of African ancestry and did not know anyone. That's when she realised she'd gone to the wrong house. The people at the house attending the funeral noticed that and helped her out.

"I've never been so ashamed and embarrassed in my life," she said, showing genuine remorse. "It's not that I have a problem mixing with any race, no that's not my problem. If those people were having a party, I would have joined in and have fun with them. My main regret is that it is a sad moment, a funeral and such occasions are not something to take lightly. I feel very bad."

The people helped this woman out of the crowd and led her up the street to wait where I was now coming to pick her up.

Now I started the vehicle and enquired where she wanted to go from here. I suggested she phone her friend which she did.

Over the conversation, she narrated that she was lost and had gone to a funeral, either in her street or somewhere near her house. On the other end of the phone, her friend admitted there was a house in the street that, for the past two days, was full of people coming and going for a funeral session. She explained to her that her house was about five blocks from the funeral house. There were a lot of people and it could be hard to drive through.

We drove right around and reached the correct house from the other end of the street and were there in less than five minutes. *Mission accomplished!* I dropped her at the right house.

As grateful as my rider was, she was also very despondent and disappointed with herself for happily walking into a funeral session holding a cake. Her sincere consolation was that she'd done it unintentionally and hoped that family had accepted her apology and would forgive her.

That was just another twist, a typical day on the road moving people around Perth metro.

Dead Drunk

On a usual early Saturday morning, about 3.30 am, I was navigating my way back into Fremantle after a drop off in Kwinana. Rather than staying in that area, I decided to head back to a known busy place with high chances of rides. Just as I was wishing for one, a call came along, and I had to divert to a house in Spearwood.

Even during such freezing early hours of the morning, I would normally expect the rider to be ready standing by the road or just by the door. From experience, I know at this time of day that all calls are from serious riders. People would be ready to go, those who got themselves drunk in the early hours would now be sober and would want nothing else but to get going. The other best part about rides and riders at this time is that most of those people don't complain about anything. They are not keen to be entertained or engaged in small talk or any of your little supposedly funny stories. They just want to go. In that regard, it is very good driving time – no unnecessary dramas at all.

So I arrived in this place and guess what I saw? No one waiting at the front: the house lights were switched off, it's early in the morning and it's cold. I looked around and up and down the street and at the houses around. There was no one to be seen.

What happens every so often is that people input the

wrong address and they can be waiting at a different house. But in this case, I did not see a soul nearby. As I was convinced no one was waiting, that it was a *no show,* as we call it, I drove into the house driveway. I intended to make a U-turn and drive away then register in the system that the pickup was a no show. Just as my headlights flashed on the front lawn, I saw some legs dangling from the garden bed. Instantly I noticed a person lying in the garden.

Like all good citizens do, I got out of the car and marched to the person, a male figure about thirty years old. He was lying flat on the ground in the recovery position. His right hand tightly gripped a quarter-full beer bottle, his other had a firm grip on a packet of cigarettes.

He was wearing jeans and a black T-shirt and was dirty all over. I walked closer, inspected him further. A mobile phone was in his side pocket and I suspected he might have called the Uber and then fallen asleep. He didn't have any injuries and was not bleeding so I concluded this was a case of drunkenness, not sickness or robbery.

I was now not sure what to do next. This was a person I had just seen at a house where I had come to pick up someone. The person in front of me was incapable of doing anything. To shake and talk to him or touch him in any way was a no! no! according to local policies.

After my visual inspection of his condition and what he was doing and, being satisfied that there was no one else to ask or talk to, I decided to ring the police. I rang the police non-emergency number and explained to them the man's condition, that I had phoned because it was very cold, and that the person may die if they didn't take him to a warmer place.

The person on the other end of the call asked me to

repeat what I'd seen, and took down the residential address. But I was told it was not an urgent case. If they had any police nearby, they would ask them to pass by and have a look.

After I had done my part, giving all the necessary details to the police, I reversed my vehicle and drove away. It was unfortunate that I could not help this guy personally and felt sorry driving away and leaving him in the cold of the morning. At least I had done my part reporting what I'd seen and handing over to the authorities responsible and qualified to handle it. I drove off with a clean and clear conscience.

The Responsible Citizen

I received a call and noted the rider was male – my assumption from the name appearing on my screen. On arrival at the pickup point I saw a male and a female standing and looking like they were waiting and ready to go. For a couple of minutes, they hugged, kissed and then waved their goodbyes. One of them, the female came into the car as the only rider.

I told her I had expected a male and showed her the name on the screen. She confirmed and assured me that it was correct, and she was the right rider.

Taking her word, I started the trip, and off we went. After her confirmation, my conclusion was that maybe that man had ordered the Uber for her.

A short distance into the trip, the lady requested me to cancel the order but she would remain in the car and place another booking.

I explained to her that for me to do that I would have to stop the vehicle, cancel and wait for her to place the order.

She just shook her head and said, "OK, let's forget about it and just keep going."

From my point of view, I did not see the logic of her ordering, waiting for the Uber to come, getting into the vehicle, then requesting to cancel and rebook the same vehicle she is already riding in.

I decided to get clarification but presenting the request

needed well-structured diplomacy.

At last, I politely asked her what the logic of the request to cancel and rebook was?

She explained that when she wanted to order this Uber her phone had lost connection and she could not place the booking through her account. After several attempts, the order still couldn't get through.

That was when this other man at the function offered to order the ride for her.

This explained the reason why her order had a male name as the rider identification. She confessed to having just met the guy at the function and did not know him well.

According to her, the right thing to do is to order your own ride rather than having someone pay for your personal expenses. I saw that as a good explanation why she had requested me to cancel the ride. All she wanted was to place the order in her name and the cost of the ride to be deducted from her account.

I expressed my appreciation for such a thought and the consideration of not taking advantage of other people. How much we would make the world a better place if we all had such a line of thinking.

In turn, she thanked me for such a nice compliment.

We travelled the rest of the trip without much talking as she was quiet and kept to herself. Quietly I was thinking to myself that this was one good citizen who did not believe in taking advantage of other people.

A bad-hearted person would have taken advantage of their expenses being paid by someone else, but this lady was out there to do all she could to avoid the expense going to someone else. What a great citizen. I wish I could also have this same type of thinking, mentality, and way of doing things. If we could all do that, how good is that?

The Annoyed Girlfriend

It was about 4.00 am when I drove out to pick up some people at a nightclub in Kwinana. On my arrival at the pick-up spot I saw three people very casually chatting who did not look like they were ready to go. Two ladies and a gentleman, a typical after-drink gathering and chatting outside the premises, laughing, hugging and a general social round off.

From my distance in the car, I could see it was pure social talk, facilitated and accelerated by the previously consumed drinks, I supposed. I waited for a while expecting someone from that group of three to come to the car for their ride, but none of them made a move.

On the opposite side of the road, I saw someone sitting alone in the dark bus shed, but did not take much notice of this person because I was looking around in anticipation of someone coming to the car from the three people standing close to where I had parked. Unfortunately, they were not ready to make a move, which led me to doubt that they were my expected riders.

Instead of wasting time, I made a quick decision to call the rider. After one ring the phone was picked up on the other side. As I tried to explain that I was the driver waiting to pick them up, I turned my head in the middle of the conversation and saw one person from the group of three on the phone casually walking towards my car. I instantly guessed that person to be the one I was waiting for.

I was surprised but chose not to ask why they kept standing there without acknowledging my arrival on time.

The gentleman, a medium built man in his thirties, clad in jeans, leather jacket, and a cap, strolled across to the car. Flinging open the front passenger door, he pulled up his jean trousers from the knees, got into the car and made himself comfortable on the seat.

As always expected, I went through the process of confirming he was the right person by asking his name to see if it matched what was on my screen.

This very jovial fella shot in a few jokes in the confirmation process, and I was just confirming his details when the person who'd been sitting alone in the bus shed opposite started walking towards the vehicle as well. She reached the car, opened the door and quietly slid into the back seat. No greetings, no nothing.

I now had two people in the car – the caller sitting in the front and this other lady who had just walked in sitting at the back. On inquiry of what was going on, the caller confirmed that she was his girlfriend. I didn't want to ask but thought it awkward that this man was flirting with these other two ladies when his girlfriend was sitting lonely in the street bus shelter. Meanwhile, his girlfriend just sat there quiet and collected, not saying anything.

While this man confirmed this lady was his girlfriend, one of the two ladies left behind from the group came to his window and asked if she could come along and share the trip with them.

Before she'd even finished her request, the man, without a second thought, flatly and rudely rejected her request – one of those typical unfriendly dismissals – a typical 'go away' rejection.

The lady, on receiving the awkward decline of her polite request, instantly poured out to him a few unspeakable words which I pretended not to hear – not nice words which caused a fair bit of discomfort for us all. After that the (bulky) fattish lady sauntered away in an exaggerated gait, pushing her hips excessively sideways, complimented by her swinging long arms with excessive dangling jewellery. Nothing to do with me, I pretended not to hear or see anything.

Then before I started the trip the girlfriend from the back seat just lost it and started verbally insulting the man, accusing him of hugging and kissing the woman whose request he had just declined.

In self-defence, the man denied outright ever kissing or hugging her, throwing back a question to polish up his innocence. "How could I ever do that in your presence?"

"Yes, you did!" she exploded at the top of her voice, her anger, frustration, and annoyance fully apparent.

I couldn't help pretending not to hear what was happening, but just kept quiet and let the drama unfold.

"Now let's go," said the man, which I happily did at once.

He then requested that we go past a McDonald's drive-through. That was fine with me. At the same time, he asked the girlfriend in the back seat what she wanted to order. Sad to say that, in that same high-pitched voice, she said, "No, I don't want nothing from you. I just want to go home!"

I could see her through the rear-view mirror leaning forward, wide-eyed and pointing at the man emphatically.

I could feel the tension in the car but kept quiet, kept my neutral stance and concentrated on my driving.

I enjoyed it when the man took up some natural

negotiation skills to control the volatile situation. The indirect apology, sweet and soft response to the high-pitched angry responses and keeping himself calm and collected. He suggested that she got some food, even if she didn't want to eat now, that she might be hungry later. He expressed his understanding that she was a bit angry now but would not like to see her hungry later.

"Food is very important especially after a good night out like we've just had," he soothed her.

He then snuck in an apology during his brief peace lecture. Then he requested me to pull over and stop the vehicle, which I did as there was space on that stretch of the road to safely stop. Not sure of his intentions, he opened the door, climbed out of the vehicle and went to sit at the back with the girlfriend. We resumed the trip.

Peace, at last, it seemed as they lowered their voices and seemed to agree. The lady accepted his apology. I followed the bend and pulled the vehicle into the McDonald's drive-through. Coincidentally, Bob Marley's hit song *One Love* playing on my Google music playlist, the sound blended in perfectly with that desired moment of peace.

They both ordered their meals. Then the lady softly said, "Please order something for the driver."

Just to go with the happy and peaceful flowing atmosphere in the car, I requested a small frozen Coke. The orders came quickly and we took off to their destination. I enjoyed watching the volatile situation being controlled and the final happy peaceful ending.

We safely arrived and they both gave their appreciation for the drive, happily climbed out and we waved our goodbyes as they happily walked up their driveway into the house.

Whatever happened thereafter, let's leave that to our imaginations.

The Gilmore College Student

I was dropping off in Kwinana around 6.00 pm one Wednesday evening. Just as I was about to drive off, I received a call to pick up a rider at a house near the town centre. On arrival, a young man with a satchel on his back came to the car. From his appearance, I took him for a young man going to work at one of the fast-food chains dotted all over the city.

He climbed in the front passenger side. "Good evening," he said with a respectful and dignified voice as he strapped on the seat belt.

With that initial greeting as an invitation of conversation, I was very impressed. Normally those in this age group prefer to be quiet and keep to themselves.

From the discussions we had, it reminded me not to judge a book by its cover. When this youngster came to the vehicle, I looked at him as a youngster who would not want to talk, but he up and started talking to me. How good is that!

I asked him how his day had been and what were his plans for the night – just a wide open question to broaden the talk. He went on to tell me he was coming from a friend's house. Then I asked if he was a young apprentice or still in college. Relaxed and at ease, he confirmed that he was a Year 12 student at Gilmore College in Kwinana. To suit the occasion, I threw in the various questions that suit a school-going individual – issues like his perception of the school; the school subjects' range and what he was pursuing; sports activities and what he was more interested in; what he intended to do after school etc.

My young rider guy proceeds to tell me how great his school was, all the privileges at the school regarding his career path. He said he was so happy and confident that he was one of the luckiest people to go to such a school. He told me about the Auto Electrical course the school was helping in which, when he finished his Year 12, he would go for a full apprentice programme. As a full ambassador of the school, he talked of a lot of good things the school was doing, a lot of optional programmes that were available for the students to take. And he was very grateful to be pursuing his dream career in the Auto Electrical trades with the full backing of his school.

At the same time, he lamented that most of his colleagues at the school did not see those opportunities which were right in front of them. But for him, even if he failed to carry on with his career ambition, he was sure that all the opportunities were laid out and that he would never come back to blame the school. He was in full support of the school extra curriculum activities and preparation for the students' life after school.

We arrived at his destination and as this very polite and confident young man left the car and we said our goodbyes, I looked at him with full admiration.

How some people from any group are so focused. How other people can see what many others around them are not seeing – bright and intelligent and not out there to blame any circumstantial situations, but wide-eyed to see the best out of whatever is there.

This young man was so determined to pursue his

career and at his age was fully in support of his school and was talking very positively about the institution.

I drove off thinking how the school authorities should know they had such responsible and focused youngsters in their midst. A classic ambassador of Gilmore College, a good modern school in Kwinana, one of Perth's southern suburbs.

FIFO Got Dumped

At 3.30 am I went to pick up at a house in central Byford. I have always liked calls and pickups at such a time. They are from serious riders and they are always long rides.

I arrived at the place and saw one guy standing in the driveway. Without wasting time, he came straight to the car. I checked his identity for confirmation, all was good, and we hit the road.

As I started the trip, I noticed the destination was Mandurah. That was a good one because that's a pretty long trip. The guy sat down with a water bottle in his arms, relaxed, calm and collected.

For a short while, I did not engage him in small talk, but the atmosphere remained free and relaxed. I could tell he was a likable and approachable person, someone with a good and friendly personality.

To set the small talk ball rolling, I eventually asked how his night had been, and where he was going at such an early hour of the day.

Casually he told me his full story, which went like this:

He'd been out for the night just to refresh his mind and to gain his composure again.

When he used the word *again*, I grew curious to know what had happened. Why would someone like him have 'gain his composure again'? This is the abridged version of what my rider said.

"Mate, I was out there to refresh myself," he said. "The house where you pick me up is my friend's place. This guy had invited me to go out. I came to his house and then the three of us, me, himself and his wife went out to Northbridge in the city.

"Somehow something happened between them in Northbridge, and the wife got a taxi and went home alone. That was about 9:10 pm," he said.

"Now this time, about 3.00 am, me and my mate got an Uber to his place. We got there and the wife didn't want to open the doors. All the doors are locked, the guy is calling her mobile and the wife is not picking up. We've been standing there for the last 45 minutes outside in the cold; can you imagine that.

"Then finally this guy breaks one of the windowpanes to have access into the house. And all along I'm standing there. I can't do anything because I've not been invited and it's not my place. I just had to stand and watch. When this guy got entry into the house the wife came out and there was a full-on verbal war right in my presence.

"Now this is when I decided to order this Uber. When I told the guy that I'd just ordered an Uber and I wanted to go to my place, he tried to get me to stay but I'd seen enough, and I didn't want to be there anymore. And right now, I am going to my place."

Then he goes:

"The real thing is that I just broke off with my girlfriend this past week. We have been together for eight years. We are both FIFO and we are hardly home at the same time. It is always a hard time to see each other. Now my girlfriend has just called it quits, she said that's it, the affair is not working well for us. The love is no longer there.

"So right now, I am in the process of recovery.

Therefore, this guy had invited me to his house just to entertain me or to refresh me to help me come back to my feet. And now this happens: he is now in big trouble with the wife. Maybe the wife doesn't want me to hang out with him? That did not help me going to his place. What then do I do? I can't just sit and stare in the air and witness the quarrelling.

"It's not fun to imagine that I've just been dumped by my girlfriend and left alone stranded. We've been together for eight years, and I've never cheated on her, now she just decided to go.

"Then this happens again tonight. What a mess. Anyway, I am better off go to my house and rest and forget about everything, it's not my moment right now."

Throughout his narrative I kept quiet, listening and imagining. I could tell that he was telling me just to get it off his chest, the idea of saying something to someone who's willing to listen. At the same time, I was very much aware that I'm not maybe the best person to be told such a very personal story. I am not in the best position to advise what to do. My role, I felt, was to sympathise with him. I also knew that I had to be very cautious if I decide to open my mouth and say anything about what I'd just been told.

The Spiked Drink

You must read this one with a very open mind. Anyone can ask the question, what's the big deal about that? Anyone who pays good attention to this and passes it on in their circles will be doing a lot of good in the community.

After the encounter I challenged myself with the question, how could I have stopped that?

Maybe there is not much I could have done since I was on my driving duties and it was out of my customer liaison responsibility. I am supposed to pretend I did not see or hear anything. Still, there is room to do better with such cases in future. Writing about it, I hope will go a long way to educate a lot out there.

I went to pick up this teenage passenger from Armadale, going to Kenwick.

The time was 6.30 pm on a Friday. Yes, usual time for weekend functions. He comes to the car smartly dressed in a colourful sweater, baseball cap dropping on the right side of the head, demin black jeans and sparkling blue and white striped sports shoes. In his right hand was a two-litre breakfast juice plastic container with a light-brownish beverage in it.

That was all my quick survey of him and the goods he was carrying managed as he came into the car.

A nice mannered young man, according to my instant judgment. This I derived from his initial engagement with me as he sat down, and I swiped the trip start button. I quickly went on to enquire about his Friday night agenda.

With a toothy smile, he giggled and explained to me that all was set for this birthday party he was going to. He was not sure what time he intended to come back.

"I will go with the flow," he said.

"And your drink?" I asked since the drink he was carrying did not really match a Friday night gig beverage criteria.

That's when I heard all about it, and of course to my utter surprise since I least expected what came out of his mouth.

He admitted that it was not the original juice in it. He had just garnished it up with a dash of vodka and brandy.

"Why is that?" I asked even though I did not know the proportions of the said spirits used for the so-called garnished beverage. It just seemed to me like it was an evil intent to let other people drink spirits without their knowledge.

"This is to wake up those snobbish party-goers who announce that they don't drink. This mixture will take care of such smart people," he finished off with a laugh.

"Yep, that's how it works," he added, holding up and looking at the garnished drink with admiration as though it was a major anticipated party attraction.

"This is why people should always bring their own drinks to parties," I said.

"Exactly!" he added. "If you come to a party expecting to feed on other people's little goodies, this is exactly what you get!" He smiled as he looked at his cocktail, like it was a marvellous creation.

He went on and on about his drink and added that "There was nothing new about it. It's a known game and has been doing that for a long time."

To justify his actions, he told me some episodes of similar tricks in the past, and how funny it always was to see the non-drinkers getting inebriated from nowhere after the consumption of free party beverages.

"It's really good fun," he said innocently.

We finally ran out of time for further talk about this party drink as we pulled up at the party venue, his destination. A good number of people were already mingling and standing in small groups of twos and threes, almost everyone holding a drink. Music from the speakers perched on stands giving a vibe to the Friday night party fun. All sorts of cars were randomly parked around the yard.

I dropped my spiked drink passenger and he disappeared into the group clinging on to his freshly brewed cocktail.

This was my first ever time to witness someone with such a plan or rather with such an off-tangent sense of humour. I have been to several parties and have never suspected any invited person to be up to such mischief. Lucky for me I have never been spiked, but that night opened my eyes to a whole new world of suspicion.

That was an eye-opener encounter, and this story is a good warning to parents and any other party-goers. This is something that can happen anywhere and to anyone.

If you are a drinker, you can surely handle it. If you are not and you go to a party for purely social reasons and this happens to you, you will regret it for a very long time. Alcohol, especially spirits and cocktails if you are not used to them, are a quick and easy way to pull the pig out of anyone.

So, be warned. Always go to parties with your own

drink. Or drink what you know or what you are familiar with in terms of taste, smell, and colour. Otherwise, you and I can be victims if we get caught up in downing drinks we don't even know who brought them and what they are. That leads to another warning, look out for cocktails brought in by any good Samaritan!!

After all, why drink what you don't know, and what you did not buy? You have been warned!

Let's Keep it Professional

The clock had just struck midnight. My position, Hillarys, one of the popular Perth northern suburbs. That's about a good forty-minute drive from Perth inner city. I had just dropped off a nice elderly couple visiting Perth from Brisbane.

I had picked them up at the domestic airport, a comedian couple who took turns to pour out endless life stories throughout the forty-five-minute trip. Now I was contemplating driving back empty or staying put.

I decided to park myself at the Boat Harbour Marina overlooking the vast Indian Ocean covered by the complete darkness of the night. A very quiet night, a nice, quiet suburb with the noise of breaking waves hitting the stone and concrete retaining wall of the shore. The dotted lights of ships, yachts, and boats anchored out in the sea, the bright lights of the marina and the car park with numerous parked cars and boats gave me a sense of security in numbers.

Regardless, it is relatively a safe area, only the solitude of the night brings in a distant fear of the unknown.

The smell of the air from the ocean breeze and the low temperatures of the night made me leave my car engine running and turn up the heater.

I budgeted myself fifteen minutes on that spot. If

nothing came within that time I was prepared to shoot off to the city where there were higher chances of riders who were ready to go home from the night gigs.

In a space of about five minutes luck came my way – a call came in. The pick-up point was five minutes' drive from my current location.

I did not even bother to swipe my navigation to go to that place because I knew the area well. A second good glance at the location, I shot off in automatic mental navigation and was at the spot in no time.

On arrival, I pulled my Elantra up to the driveway. A well-gated and secured place with enough external lighting to impress, provide security and add a touch of beauty to the place. Professionally manicured lawns and landscaped front yard surrounded a classy, very impressive double-storey house clearly in view from the driveway. On both sides of the house were massive houses of similar description, a perfect fit.

Two expensive-looking cars were parked out the front. In no time I saw my rider coming out of the house. He squeezed past the two parked cars, and slid out through the side gate and straight to my car which was waiting on the footpath edge of the driveway.

The man, aged between 35 to 40 years, walked straight to my car, latching the gate behind him. He opened the door and dumped himself on the front seat. Well-dressed, smart casual, nice leather jacket, a pair of jeans, nice footwear and holding nothing – it was just him, as simple as that.

From experience, I could tell he was someone with lots of stories, or rather, someone you could quickly engage in any sort of conversation. A well-dressed gentleman who came in with a fresh fragrance ready for a night out. As he came in, I mistook him for someone who was coming from a friend's place for the night and now going back to his house.

No alcohol or cigarette smell, a typical smart individual. He shouted: "Let's do it!!"

This said, he strapped his belt on. I held onto my excitement of the new jolly rider and confirmed his identity before taking off. With a friendly broad smile, he said "Who can order an Uber for fun this time of the day. Yes, it's me, mate, let's go!"

The broad smile and the cheerful reply assured me I was in good company, one of those happy riders to have in your car.

This was one of those moments where you meet a rider and instantly you connect. I swiped to start the trip and the destination was The Crown Casino. What a stroke of luck, that was exactly what I was hoping for. A long drive that would take me out of this suburb straight into the busy hub of the city fringe and the Crown Casino was a perfect destination.

I started by complimenting him for such a choice as the casino for a late night out. It was a decent place and open for 24 hours, so there was no rush and at any time it is a hive of activity, full of people and lots of events to engage in. He did not rush to reply but gave a small laugh, shook his head and said, "I will keep it professional."

I decided to keep it professional.

From that small talk and that unusual phrase, I knew there was a bit of juicy news to come out. With the forty-minute drive ahead of us I knew there was plenty of time to hear all about it.

He started by telling me that he was walking out of a volatile situation.

"Oh no, that's sad," I stressed sympathetically.

"This is exactly what happened," he started his story. "We had visitors with us at the house. They came around 6:30 pm with their two teenage boys, same age as ours."

From that point I suspected that contrary to my original guess, that the fellow wasn't coming from a friend's place – he was coming from his own house.

"Throughout the visitors' stay, we were happy and throwing in jokes and humorous stories. I don't know where, but at some point, I must have thrown in a joke that did not go well with my wife and she is at war with me after the departure of the visitors. The house is in a mess; it's all nasty, no happiness; no nothing. The best thing I've decided is to walk out for the night and come back home after 6.00 am and just keep everything professional."

Seriously I must deal with it professionally. That is the only way to go.

I'm telling you the best way to go and keep everything under control is to keep it professional in the home. Maybe we must talk when there is something necessary to talk about. Whether there's a visitor or not that is the professional way to go.

As he paused in his narration, I realised this was a sensitive area. I felt privileged to be told such a private issue. Inside me, I battled to imagine 'what is professional in a relationship'. What is professional about talking to your wife, your partner or kids? I empathised but I agreed with him. I also complimented the idea of walking away for the sake of calming down and coming back home when you are cool and collected. In whatever you see and do, you will be normal and not doing anything you will regret later.

The long forty-minute trip cruising down Graham

Farmer Freeway was made shorter by the seriousness of the talk. In no time we were on the grounds of the Crown Casino and then navigating to the official drop off points. There were lots of cars parked all over the place. A very busy place with Ride-shares, taxis coming in and out, people walking all over the place, a squad of security guards controlling traffic and people is the daily routine of the place. That business hype of the casino brought in a feeling of joy and happiness. I did not want to put up any comments on this professional talk. All I did was praise him for coming to a place like this which will help him adjust his way of thinking and responding. Such time off may be the best way to settle down a bit. By the time he decided to go back home, he would be in a better state of mind. When he arrived home, he could be in a better position to administer his professional strategy in the best possible way.

He left the car with both of us agreeing that the professional approach was the best way. However, on my part, I kept struggling to comprehend what is professional in a relationship.

As I dropped him and found my way out of the buildings to go find another parking spot to wait for new rides, I kept thinking of the long trip discussion. It came back to my mind that his professional talk was more of a poetic phrase.

It's a very good talk and approach in life. It means a lot. Yes, let's keep it professional at home.

My conclusion was that this can be from what we say and what we do to each other. How our actions impact on the others can be the professional approach he was talking about.

The main conclusion on the professional talk was that

anything that will harm the other in any way, as in physically, morally and spiritually, is what we should be on the lookout for. Even in social set up, on our own or with guests, the stories we talk about and the jokes we throw around can be an insult to our better partners if we do not calculate what we say and do, hence the talk of professional building in relationships

Yes, I agree with my rider: there is a need for a professional dealing in most of what we do in relationships.

Unique Lifestyle

Over time I have picked up a lot of people doing Fly-in-Fly-out jobs, those people who work in remote areas in the mining sector – they fly to work and fly back home, hence the term Fly-in-Fly-out. Like anything else you do for a long time, I came to make friends with these people. A few have become real-life friends and some ongoing regular clients. They let me know when they're coming and their air flight schedule. The long-term business relation leads to knowing each other more outside the business framework.

One of my clients – let's call him Traveller – is a real character and a perfect case study. A very nice guy, Australian born and bred, he grew up in Cairns Queensland, he told me – a cool charming hard-working Irish descendant still very proud of his heritage but he has never been to Ireland. That's OK – it's common with most Australians. Traveller's a tall, slim-built, grey-haired man with now unmistakable aging signs all over.

One thing I like about him is his always-switched-on smile and the ability to joke and be hilarious in social chats. Each time I pick and drop him I know a quick laugh is on the way – one of those people who make life easy; a very good bloke.

Like the other day ... I picked him up and drove him to his temporary residence for that week away from work. On the way, he instructs me to drive past a liquor drive-through outlet.

"Let's stop here and I will pick up some Basics," he politely requested with a flashy smile.

I pulled over and he purchased the basics.

What were the basics? A carton of beer!

We laughed about it and from that day we now call any alcohol 'Basics'.

Apart from his excellent sense of humour, I came not to like his chosen unique lifestyle as I understood it more. His life can easily be described as 'all over the place'. That is how he has described his way of life to me and how I came to understand it. It caught my attention because it is not the common trend familiar with many of us.

That, however, does not qualify anyone to judge him, it is just of interest as it is out of the everyday norm.

The guy has been working in the mines since the mid-1990s, that is a long time. He's been all over Australia and overseas, especially countries within the Asia Pacific regions. In Australia, he owns no home, no house, no car, no nothing. It is just him, his mobile phone, his bank accounts, his wallet swollen with an assortment of cards, a few clothes, and two bags: a carryover backpack and a High Sierra Composite V3 Backpack Wheel Duffel.

His life floats between staying somewhere during a break from work, living at the mine during shift weeks and going anywhere during his time off. This *anywhere* means staying with friends, relatives, short term accommodation, Backpackers, Motels, Hotels, anywhere around Australia or flying to any Asian country for that short time off. After the one or two weeks of his time off, he then flies back to the mines. According to him, in his own words, he has made a lot of friends all over Australia and outside within the Asia region so at any time he has a wide option of places to go. These are the friends who will provide food, accommodation, and transport for him.

On the transport part, this is where I come in. I am one of his good friends in Perth and my role in his lifestyle is to provide him transport to and from the airport whenever he is around Perth, as one of his friends in his chosen lifestyle.

I will confess that he does not take advantage of the so-called friendship. He pays regular fees as per the going rate and here and there gives extra as thank you. In turn, he gets good service and the friendship base is intact.

The good part is that he is a regular for all these services he gets, and he is willing to pay them good money every time. So, it's a fair deal and in turn, the people are very nice, and everything seems to go well for him.

He has been doing this for a very long time, and it is now his lifestyle. If he is on break and coming to Perth, he will ring me and let me know what time his flight is landing and where he wants to go. By the time the flight lands and I pick him up, accommodation and food will be already organised. The rest will come.

Most of the city trips will involve going either to second-hand clothing shops or to budget clothes shops to buy clothes for that week. The whole lot will be chucked in some clothing recycling bin on his return to work. He then flies back with a light bag with his hygiene basics and his phone. No laundry, no ironing, no nothing.

At the mine site, he tells me that everything is provided. Food, accommodation and work clothes. Which means there is no expense, and life goes on like that. There is no need to buy anything. Bank and cash transactions will only be used when he comes to the city or flies out of the country.

So, there we go, that's the life of one of my encounters, a modern-day hunter and gatherer living an enlightened itinerant life, floating from mine-site to interstate and across borders with his whole life assets in his regular muddy haversack, and sure enough, life goes on.

What Do I Do Next?

I got myself ready to go for my normal drive on a Friday late afternoon. Anytime past midday on a Friday people can be going anywhere. There is no reason to drive to 'busy places'. People have various events to attend, some people finish their work early and some go for lunches and never return to work.

I accepted a call and dashed out for that quick local pick up two streets from my house. As I pulled up the driveway, my female rider was standing there ready to go. A middle-aged Caucasian woman still in perfect shape and looks, decent, attractive, with moderate makeup. Classy dark sunnies tucked on the head and blending well with the hair colour complemented the obvious natural eye-catching figure in a cream necklace, long-sleeved blouse and matching skintight blue jeans. Glittering rings flashed on her fingers as she grasped a brown wallet with golden lined edges from the top by both hands flat on the belly button position.

She came in and I confirmed the name before we took off.

Destination, city, distance forty-five kilometres. That's a pretty good and perfect ride. Like all such rides, life gets better and exciting if you instantly like each other. Lucky for us, she started by appreciating the quick arrival, at the same time jokingly blaming the early response and arrival.

"That was too quick, and you people don't give us enough time to get ready," she said, letting out a light, flirty, happy laugh.

In reply, I also jokingly said, "That is the modern aspect of this type of transport – please don't call us if you're not ready yet."

We both burst into friendly laughter as we approached Thomas Road and, with Byford gradually disappearing behind us, we hit the road city-bound.

We drifted into talking about the weekend's activities and at some point started gliding into her purpose of the city trip. The short distance travelled so far itself indicated that we were of equal minds and were free to talk and joke as we cruised along on the long trip ahead of us.

After a short pause and a quick think over my question, she openly told me that she was going to meet some friends from the past. One of the obvious benefits of working and living in a city you grew up and went to school in is that you have a very large group of family and friends to mix and talk with all the time.

I appreciated that as I always miss such mixing and mingling because I live far away from where I grew up and went to school. Hence, I am one of those people who do not have a group of very close people to me who I can meet and talk to regularly on a social basis. That is being lonely. You only need to be living far away from where you grew up or in a different country to experience such a feeling.

"I just want to try to meet people who can support and help me with how I can move forward," she said in a low sorrowful voice.

"Are you in a life crisis phase? Are you OK?" I enquired with a nearly similar low sympathetic voice. From her talk, and judging from the sudden vocal variation, I sensed that all was not well.

"There is more inside than what you are seeing outside right now. I must polish a few things about my life. Things are not looking good right now. I need help and the best way for me now is to go and meet these people," she expressed without hiding her gloomy expression.

"When I picked you up, I assumed you to be someone who just finished work early today and is going for a Friday afternoon catch up." I came up with a totally different strategy to ease the emotional pressure building up in her.

Looking straight forward as though she was the driver, she responded, "No, I've been sitting at home for a month now."

With all this talk she suddenly burst into laughter and announced that: "No hard feelings, no emotions. Everything will be alright." A good sudden rise into self-encouragement, she smiled widely and giggled.

We carried on with the happy chit-chat, making the trip and the conversation easy-going and enjoyable.

Casting a sharp glance at me as I was driving, she gave me a synopsis of her story.

"All my life since I was 16 when I left school," she began, "all I have done for a job is tiling, that is all I know. Now I'm in my 50s my body cannot cope with the demands to constantly lift, kneel, scrub, push, bend, crawl and all the other demands of this trade. The body can't take it anymore. It is now way too much for me," she lamented. "I'm done. I just want something different!"

Clear determination washed over her face.

"Now I'm stuck with the decision about what to do next, where can I go, what's the new thing I can do? Where and what if I want to train? What can I train in? How long will it take me to do the training? Will I get a job as age seems to be against me on completion of the training.

"That is the sort of help and advice I'm looking for, she said seriously. All I know is tiling, that's it."

After a good listening, I felt for her. I switched from a joking mood to more serious talk and quickly chipped in and applauded her for such a move.

Again, she burst into sarcastic laughter, followed by: "What do I do now!" She repeated the statement twice.

"You don't look worn out," I assured her, aiming to boost her self-esteem. That was a genuine comment: she did not look as worn out as she had described herself.

That was, of course, a candid and honest statement. From her looks, you could not conclude that she was weak or old. No, she had all the looks and attributes of a fit and healthy person with still a lot of years ahead in an active, physically demanding job.

"Yes, you can say that," she went on, "but I'm telling you right now that my body is tired. I cannot do it anymore, honestly, I do not want to lift any bricks, pavers, bags of sand or anything. I just can't do it anymore. My body is reminding me of my age and silently telling me to slow down. I regret what I have done over the years. It's not too late to change, I just want to give it a go and deal with it."

With her open and honest account of such a personal story, I added that "Life has no formula". It can be by coincidence that we end up in better career paths and some regretting their teenage years' choices. Circumstances and peers around us may play a bigger role in our choices, but in the end, it is us who dance to the tune of the later consequences of our choices.

The good and positive part of that trip was that she was going to meet past friends to brainstorm the best suitable and practical way out of her predicament. I praised her for such a bold move to seek assistance. It was always highly likely that many brains focusing on any issue, a workable, positive and practical solution would be worked out.

"I don't know what good ideas I will get from them," she said but was very optimistic and confident that someone may help her out of her seemingly downward moment.

I wished her the best and gave my thumbs up for the initiative to solve a problem.

Next, I was finding parking for a safe and nice spot to drop her at the St George's Terrace destination.

The forty-five-minute trip had gone in a flash. The talk, the laughter and the easy cruise along the Friday afternoon incident-free Kwinana Freeway made the travel nice and easy. It remained my sincere hope that she got a bargain from her Friday afternoon catchup with mates.

Like in most cases, we hear these stories, drop the person and may never meet them again. Regardless, I believe the genuine verbal good luck wishes to anyone goes a long way to inject hope and good fortune into people's lives.

Yes, I may never meet her again, but it remains my sincere hope that all went well for her.

Retired at Last

After a drop-off, I got stuck somewhere in Bullsbrook. That place is far from the maddening urban buzz, a faraway place with fewer chances of a quick possible ride back to the city. The only sensible option remains to drive the long distance back to Perth with no one on board. That has always been the disadvantage of such long trips to the outer suburban areas.

As I searched my way to the quickest route back to the city, I got a call from a pickup on the very road I was driving along. Two kilometres down the road, I was there, parked in the driveway and waiting for my rider to come out.

After a few minutes, a bold and grey-headed, physically weak-looking man came slowly out of the house, taking his time to lock the door. He was dressed in workwear pants and a worn-out brown long-sleeved khaki shirt, an old-looking Australian bush hat and untidy loose-fitting work boots.

Nice and slow, he placed his small bag in the back seat, and we exchange greetings in the process. I confirmed his name as he eased himself into the front seat, adjusted his seat and locked himself in place with the seat belt.

Bullsbrook to Ellenbrook, a good half-hour ride. *Great!* And we hit the road. A steady and soft-spoken man, his thoughts and talk structure told that he had seen a lot.

He expressed his gratitude for my early arrival in such

a far place from the inner urban hype. Normally he had to wait a long time before an Uber arrived. I explained the coincidence of my drop off in his neighbourhood.

He told me that at one point in his life he drove taxis. He assured me that he knew how hard it is to drive for a living. To boost my spirit, he encouraged me to give it my best if that is what I do for a living and is my line of survival. In addition to the encouragement, he warned me to keep an eye on the accounts section as cash comes in and out.

I assured him that I gave that responsibility to people in an accounting business so I didn't end up owing anything to the Tax Department. Again, he insisted that I still must have a close eye in all transactions, his emphasis raising my eyebrows. I threw a question to get the details of how he kept an eye on these transactions when he was driving taxis and how well he did it.

In a relaxed and cautious manner, he gave me an abridged account of his life journey.

After his Taxi driving stint, this good old man had worked all his life in the mines. He had worked all over Australia as a shutdown contractor. He'd never stayed home – home management was left to his wife, and the kids grew up in luxury but without him.

It had been a year since he'd retired. The body couldn't take it anymore. He'd admitted it was hard to compete with youngsters and it was time to call it quits. So, he'd left and was back at home in the city. The one year in retirement had revealed to him shocking revelations about the fruits of his labours.

Over the years, his life was two or four weeks away and one week at home. That was the pattern. The week at home was always resting time, home transactions, developments, renovations. Banking and all purchases and transactions such as mortgages, rates and all sorts of payments were the wife's obligations. The unwritten contract was that he went to work, brought in the money, and she managed the income and the home upkeep and development.

He admitted that he'd never kept track of money movement and transactions; had no idea of how much was coming in and how much was paid out and when. According to him, it was a system that worked and gave him no stress. On the downside, he was behind in terms of how and when transactions were done. He lacked the knowledge of the ongoing business transactions and that trend saw him left far behind.

All he knew was he had his bank card and occasionally swiped it over when he got to buy something. This arrangement ended up in a situation that everything bought was in the wife's name – cars, boats, house, and rental properties. He knew about them but was not aware of the documentation and the real ownership.

That was his work-life: working hard for big money but not dealing or managing the money and he missed out on the financial side of the family financial management. Six months into his retirement the wife got sick, deteriorated and was now in care in a home.

The kids had grown up and gone. Now all the financial responsibilities were in his hands. This was coming down on him like a massive avalanche of responsibility he had never coped with before. To get help, a friend suggested that he spoke to a financial adviser.

He took the advice and now was a very good friend of that financial advisor, a good-hearted man who had reviewed the shocking previous financial dealings in his house which he should have owned years ago. The only thing he owned was a joint bank account with his now bed-ridden old, sick wife. This gave him the ability to buy using bank cards. On the downside he owned nothing. Every asset they had as a family was either in the sick wife's name or either of the two grown-up, gone kids.

He had nothing in his name. How and when these assets were twisted without his knowledge, he had no idea.

He recalled that at one time during his active years, he had told his family that his fly-in-fly-out job was relatively dangerous. He had suggested that all their belongings be in the wife's name. If he died out there, it would be easy for the family to bypass the deceased estate legal transactions that would cost them a lot.

That was a general talk, but it was never agreed to go ahead without his knowledge. Whatever happened, the fact remained that he owned nothing.

I kept quiet all the time as I listened and absorbed his very personal, sensitive story. It was not one of those stories you jump in and carelessly add or say something to compliment the conversation. No, you must just listen and maybe take heed.

As we drew closer to his destination he briefly stopped and advised me to take a different route than the GPS was showing. Then he shook his head and cast a sharp glance at me like I was his sibling and said, "What do I do now? Where do I go for help? Who do you trust on this earth?" A very strong self-searching statement that left me cold and uncomfortable.

I just shook my head and could not say anything, then he quickly switched to more jovial talk. "That's it, mates, anything can happen; we'll see what happens!"

I pulled up to his wine brewery destination and we said

our goodbyes.

Then I drove away with his story stored in my head. One of those sad stories that can come as a hidden life lesson. It can also be an addition to life-time stories that may sound fake. We may not imagine it until such mishaps knock on our door.

The Young Electrician

On a Friday night, I picked up this young fella from Mandurah going to a get-together at the Crown Casino, a pretty long trip for a social event, I thought as the trip outlined on the GPS screen.

With his drink in hand, and casually dressed in jeans and a floral business shirt, just as we set off, he shouted, "Mission accomplished!"

"Someone must be happy," I said.

"Yes, my brother. I am one happy fellow right now. I'm really pleased with myself."

It is always encouraging to meet people who kick off initial engagement with such positive talk. It sets the two of you straight into a good mood and you both look forward to the trip and joyous conversation. Apparently, this young rider of mine had worked in the mines for a decade, since the age of 21, he told me.

"I'm very proud of my dad who gave me a lecture on how to make your own life plan. I followed that and now it has paid dividends," he said.

I chipped in with a quick question about his dad's advice, keen to know what tips he'd followed and what dividends the advice had yielded.

It was not common for young lads to take their parents' words of advice, and this was one case I was so keen to hear what was said and how he did it.

Normally at that age, everything was happening and was always a regret when we looked and thought about how we would have done it differently.

"Yes, I did it, mate. I paid close attention as my dad was advising me," he said. "I got a job in the mines and went in there with a well-thought work strategy and a list of things to buy and acquire and a clear exit plan. That is exactly what I did," the young man told me.

"That is very good and encouraging to hear. How did the plan go? Did you manage to tick all the boxes?" I inquired.

With confidence and a clear voice, he gave me a brief account of his accomplishments which sounded very impressive: in his ten-year fly-in-fly-out job he had married his high school sweetheart. That was the first tick and first step to real adulthood. By a stroke of good fortune, according to him, he married gold, a down-to-earth girl ready to be a wife and mother. Together they were a perfect combination of the same mindset, direction, and life focus.

They had built houses; had kids and all the necessary luxury toys were in place. In the last two years before his mine job exit, he had set up a business that had taken off perfectly since he came home from the mines.

With advertisements floating in the local paper and on social media, Perth being spread out, he concentrated on the south side and did very well, according to him.

"That was the plan," he said, flashing a broad smile and displaying a positive posture of a high achiever.

"Now mission accomplished, properties are in place, wife, kids, toys, business and most of all I am still young and will be home every night with my wife and kids," he added.

I was sitting there listening to this and my conclusion was, "Another brilliant young mind well organised and focused."

How we all have it but some will shine more than others. We arrived at his Crown drop of point and I let go my happy achiever and carried on with my night driving duties.

Silently, I pondered how good luck and fate in life randomly pick people. At that age I was nowhere near there – blessed are the two who brought up such an admirable young, responsible and focused citizen.

The Booze Bus/The Sober Driver

It was after midnight and I picked up a middle-aged couple from Fremantle, going to Applecross. They must have been coming from a dinner function with friends. You need not be told that they were not fit to drive. Yes, you guessed it.

The lady was a non-stop chatty, happy woman, well dressed for an outing, with a stylish hairdo and dangling sparkling gold and silver in ears, wrist, and fingers. The man straight away starts humming a song at a low and deep voice despite the music in the car. The lady says in a loud clear voice, "Just do your thing. Safely drive us home as we are both over the limit and tonight you are our last hope, buddy!"

She finished with a big laugh and happily threw herself back on the seat and gave the husband a soft, well-calculated, flirtatious push.

The humming husband raised his head and added, "Yes, we can't drive lest we get ourselves in trouble."

I then realised they had driven to the function but were now getting Uber because they knew their legal limits and their current status. The wife then threw in a joke about me.

"We sincerely hope we are in very safe hands. We left our car behind to be driven home by this lovely man. If by any chance we get pulled over by the police and this seemingly happy, sober-looking driver of ours is deemed to be over the limit, that shall be news headlines."

We all burst into laughter. Even the husband, who was in his own world humming the unknown song, threw himself up in glee, and in song responded: "It's too late, my darling, we are already at risk."

Again, more merriment and joyous laughter erupted from all in the vehicle.

To add to the happy mood, I chipped in with a Rap-like rhythm response.

"I the good driver!
Confess that, that!
You, you are all!!
All in safe hands, Yeeh!
Because your driver is,
Yee! Yoo!!
A sober man
Yee!! Yee!!!

That sealed it. With my natural deep voice, they enjoyed it. The chatty wife liked the quick impromptu Rap song, and just as quick after the laughter asked that I do it again. As a song I had just made up from nowhere I could not recall all the words nor the rhythm I'd used. So I suggested we all sing it together and the combined sound of our three voices would give a good and joyous musical output.

Just as we were in the middle of all that song polish up, we approached a long stretch of road, a hill on one side and a bowling club on the other, a good stretch of road with no other roads to branch off or to make a quick U-turn. Right there in front of us, was flashing blue lights and cars jammed up bumper to bumper.

The narrow road, a sea of red from brake lights as the

vehicles slowed down, then crawled and stopped. Who needed to be told what that was in the middle of the night? A clear sign, white on blue was strategically placed for all drivers to read and prepare for what was ahead.

ANYTIME ANYWHERE
DRINK DRIVING
STOPS HERE!!

We all went quiet and stopped the singing game, preparing for what was ahead. The lady passenger whispered, "Oops, the moment of truth we were just talking about."

No-one replied. We all went quiet. I slowed the car and followed the directions of one of the police officers. It was a spectacle: cars moving slowly on both sides of the road; every single driver being breath tested; Police cars everywhere with their blue and red lights flashing; male and female officers in their trademark colours.

Glittering yellow reflective jackets and an assortment of military hardware clung on black leather belts around their waistlines. A Police special bus (booze bus) parked up for second testing those who were over the limit on the first reading. A few cars were parked off the road and the drivers and passengers looked miserable. Whatever fate awaited them was the last expectation for us.

I opened a bottle of water and gulped a good mouthful. I was just thirsty, that's all. Looking at me at an angle from his side of the back seat the man whispered in a surprised voice, "Don't tell me you are drunk, mate!" He looked straight at me. His voice, posture, and expression turned the previous jovial state to a more serious and near angry look.

"All good. No, I'm not," I assured them.

One police officer controlling the movement of traffic

directed me to the centre position. I stopped and lowered my window, awaiting my turn. With the testing instruments in his hand – a plastic barrel-shaped 15-centimetre pipe, the officer told me to blow into the tube until he said 'Stop'.

"Yes, let's do it," I wholeheartedly agreed.

I blew in hard and ran out of breath. The Officer was far from impressed by that. "A man like you can do better than that," he said in a less than friendly tone.

The Officer, a short, stout and strong-looking man who looked like he has seen it all before, slowly instructed me to blow in again until he told me to stop. For the second time, I gave it another hard push and kept going again. I was out of breath but just hung in there. It's funny how air just runs out, gone, nothing, and you are almost fainting. I guess that's the same feeling you go through when you are drowning.

Just as I was about to give up and gulp another bout of fresh air, the police officer came to my rescue. "Stop," he instructed authoritatively.

In the meanwhile, cars were slowly moving, officers and other people going up and down. That small moment plus the people in the car all seem to be saying, "What have we done?"

The officer looked at the instrument, took off the white pipe and brown part and handed it to me as a souvenir. He looked at me and the passengers like he was seeing us for the first time.

"You are good to go, all clear. Drive safely."

Done and clear, good responsible driver. I was proud of myself. The trip continued with my two back seat passengers instantly falling asleep after the breath testing moment. Maybe it was from the assurance that they were in the hands of a sober and responsible driver.

Another six kilometres' drive and we were at their destination. They woke from their mini sleep as I pulled into the driveway.

I safely dropped them and we said our goodbyes.

The man pointed at me saying, "Keep doing a good job."

The lady finished off with: "That was a close call. Lucky you didn't drink today," speaking as though she'd known me for drinking anywhere in the past. Again, we chuckled for the last time.

With that last laugh they disembarked and staggered up to their house and I continued with my night driving job.

Nice People Out There

It is always the negative we are quick to complain about, but if you look closely around any community you will be amazed at the number of very nice people out there. Anytime, anywhere, you are bound to bump into someone very nice to your utter surprise.

Apart from the negative encounters, I've also bumped into unforgettable moments of politeness, forgiving, and help from many riders. Strange and rare as they may be, yes people can do a lot of nice deeds and when they go, you are left wondering if it was a strategy to get something from you. No, just ordinary everyday people choosing to be nice, giving a helping hand and being considerate to those providing them with a service.

In Mandurah on a Saturday morning, this call came about 4.30 am. The call came about four times and the rider kept cancelling each time I accepted. About the fifth time calling, I realised it was from the same person. I waited for a while, just in case I picked it up and they cancelled again. Finally, I pushed the accept button, swiped the navigation and I was on my way to the pickup point.

All the way I was preparing myself for them to cancel again. Regardless of my pessimism, I just kept going, and thinking ahead about our encounter. From experience, I knew that the trip could be horrible if for some strange reason we instantly didn't like each other. I have been through this a lot of times. Whatever their reason for continuous cancelation, I know not to ask why. I just pick them up quietly and then safely drive them wherever they are going. Don't make people feel bad, pretend you don't know, and everyone is happy.

At the pick-up point, I saw a middle-aged Asian lady standing on the driveway as I pulled up; she was clearly restless and ready to go.

Without delay, I picked her up and off we went. My GPS indicated a good ten minutes' drive. She sat quietly in the back seat and I did not bother her with any small talk – from my assessment, she was not in the mood for a laugh.

In the last three minutes of the trip, she said she was restless and worried because she was already late for work. When she placed her order, my GPS indicated that I was more than fifteen minutes away, which was why she kept cancelling the order. She thought she could get another Uber within five minutes of her pickup point. Unfortunately, at that time of the day, it is hard to get cars as most drivers would be tired and have gone home. At that moment I was the only driver in that area, and she had to wait. This explained why she kept cancelling the call when they came to my phone and I was fifteen minutes away – a very good reminder why we should never rush to think negatively when riders cancel their requests.

The good point was that she was very apologetic and even thanked me for coming to pick her up. In this case, even though she was late she did not bother me to speed up. Her cancellations were nothing sinister but just trying to get a car nearest her. All along the trip she was nice and quiet and spoke to me with every ounce of respect. How nice and respectful some people among us are, and how I wish to do the same to others.

On other occasions, I have dealt with some very nice people, polite people who give a very challenging positive attitude, instances like picking up someone who addresses you as Sir! When they want anything from refreshment mints and water in the car or a decent request like to stop over at Maccas for a quick bite to eat in the car or take-away, or anything. They ask and start with the magic phrase "Please". Even some drunken riders, while aware of their drunken state, still give that soothing approach to requests and sincerely apologise for any mishaps.

In this job of driving people around, mistakes are bound to happen, such as missing a freeway off-ramp, or a wrong turn into a suburban street or navigation other than the rider's preferred route. Some people will take it in and help you to get back on track with little or no blame. They don't rush to accuse and will go out of their way to help rectify genuine mistakes. I very much like nice people – they help make life easy and puts you in a positive mood which challenges you to even do better and be nicer to the next person.

How good is that! How about we all try to make being nice go viral and spread it quick like wildfire. What a difference that would make to the world we live in and share.

Lady Misses Her Flight

From Perth International Airport I picked up a middle-aged lady of African descent and her teenage daughter, going to Joondalup. They were very nice, soft-spoken and polite. From the initial conversation, we quickly picked up each other's accents and instantly the communication diverted from English to an African language, *Shona*.

When I asked where she was coming from, she did not want to go into the details of what had happened, but abruptly answered, "We missed our plane and now we are going back to stay overnight with relatives."

The amount of luggage with them suggested they must have been coming from somewhere far away, or coming from a long holiday.

Just as she finished telling me that she'd missed her plane, the daughter joined in the conversation and said, "Mum, we did not miss our plane – the flight was cancelled."

The mother laughed it off then explained that she did not want to bother me with all the details. She went on to say that she disliked the outback lifestyle where flights are always cancelled if the passenger numbers are low.

Now they were faced with a double expense – the cost of the current trip and another return trip back to the airport the next day. Above all, there was the disruption to people's routines as they were going to stay with relatives

Just as we were in the middle of the conversation, her phone rang. She picked it up and I turned the car radio volume down. The phone was on such a high volume I could hear her conversation. It was her husband on the phone and they started conversing in that African language. On the other end, the husband assumed that the Uber driver could not understand their conversation. The lady told him of the flight cancellation and her disappointment about that. She explained they were in an Uber going back for another overnight stay with relatives, and that the flight was rescheduled for the next day.

The husband rushed on to caution her to keep an eye on the Uber drivers as they can opt for a long route and take advantage of them because you don't know the place.

The bad news was that the conversation was quick, and the wife did not have time to brief the husband about the driver. It was a classic *faux pas*. You are aware that a third party is hearing and can understand your conversation. The other person keeps talking sending you into further embarrassment. To soften the situation, I put the radio volume up a bit and pretended I was not hearing any of their conversation.

I could feel an intense atmosphere in the car as she avoided commenting on the husband's suggestions but kept switching the subject and line of discussion.

On completion of the conversation, an awkward silence blanketed us. The daughter at the back seat broke the silence when she asked, "What did Dad say to you, Mum?".

The mother scrambled for an appropriate answer to put her at ease and to help her out of the embarrassing response about the phone conversation. I suggested they stay at a hotel close to the airport than the forty-five-minute ride to Joondalup, which was going to be more expensive for them.

"I'm ok to make a U-turn and go to a hotel close to the airport," I said.

That was a solution I thought would get them out of the suspicion of a con Uber Driver trying to get a long-distance drive as the husband had suspected. She then asked me to stop as she wanted to make a phone call to her husband about the airport accommodation suggestions. I complied.

When the husband picked up the phone, she got out of the car for a private chat far from my earshot – I suspect that she told him that I could understand their language.

After her brief consultation with the husband, she returned to the car and told me they had agreed that we continue with the trip to the original destination. The daughter would spend another night with her cousins, and they would be in a relaxed and familiar environment.

We continued the rest of the journey with both parties trusting each other. Contrary to the thought of ripping them off, the Uber driver was an everyday honest man, just picking and dropping people regardless of distance.

With no incidents and a nice and smooth ride, the long trip to Joondalup turned out to be great as we had a lot of familiar subjects to talk about and had language and country of origin in common.

We don't take advantage of anyone, but endeavour to offer help and aim to deliver a memorable ride experience.

Goodbye Sweetie

Day and time: Sunday, 4.30 am. I went to pick up in Gosnells Hills. At that early hour I thought and expected the call to be a quick airport run.

I branched off Tonkin Highway and hit the road up into the hills. A few turns and curves later, I was at my destination.

A man and a woman were already waiting on the driveway.

Both were casually dressed. The man carried a 2-litre breakfast juice in his hand; the woman was on the phone and wearing an oversized grey jacket and carried a sagging multi-coloured hand-crafted woollen handbag hanging from the right shoulder. With her messy hairdo and no visible make-up, it occurred to me they were carefree people who were unconcerned about what the world thought of them. They were just there, ready to go, that's it.

The man quickly pulled and puffed long breaths of his e-cigarette as the woman opened the back door and made herself comfortable in the back seat. The thick escaping cloud of the e-cigarette shot out from his mouth like the exhaust smoke from a jet plane. On completion of the smoke exhalation, the guy sat in the front with me, his hand still clinging to his 2-litre breakfast juice.

I lowered the windows to refresh the air. In the back,

the lady busily searched in her handbag.

"Oh, my wallet and glasses!" she screamed in a low tone.

The man, without even turning his head to look at her, responded, "Don't worry. I will bring them to you later."

"Oh, thank you, Sweetie," she said affectionately.

In the front, I noticed the breakfast juice in the guy's hand was half-full and held casually but he was not drinking it. He was grasping it to himself and not in the slightest mood to share.

We rolled down the hill towards Kelmscott and enjoyed the night city views from our higher location. The Elantra slid down past the big trees and the large country-style properties up in the hills. Finally, we were down in the valley; we crossed the river; drove up the windy road and onto Dan Murphy around about and then hit a sharp left into Albany Highway, Kelmscott.

It was Sunday morning and the roads were quiet and empty. Typical suburbs far from the city, only five-metre-high pole streetlights and their bright illumination and the few colours from the petrol stations are pleasures to the eye and nothing much else to see.

Up to this point in the trip, these two people are not talking. I broke the silence by asking a few open-ended questions. Instead of answering my questions, the lady decides to override the GPS and started navigating for me.

In the name of customer service, I chose to ignore the GPS and followed her instructions. In the past I have learnt the hard way in disregarding a rider's preference to navigate themselves. That was a good idea as it got her to talk.

We drove past Spud Shed on the right, past the traffic

lights and then another sharp left past McDonald's and Sizzlers restaurant on the right. A few metres from Brookton Highway and I was asked to stop. Just stop. No house. No shop. No nothing. She opened the door, tapped the guy on the shoulder and said, "Goodbye, Sweetie."

With her handbag hanging on her shoulder, not even looking back for a last wave, she walked away along the suburban roadside walkway. Likewise, the man acted similarly, just kept looking forward like he was the driver. No goodbye, no wave, no nothing.

Down along the street, she paced like she was not yet at her destination.

I swiped down my Uber App phone screen to confirm the completion of the first stop of the trip, and the second phase of the trip continued with the guy to the next destination.

"Looks like she is still walking. Why didn't we drop her at the exact address?" I quizzed the man.

"I don't know, it was her choice. I think she lives around here," he replied casually, clearly not caring.

"What do you mean? She was saying all that sweetie sweetie talk to you and you are telling me you don't know where she lives," I cautiously inquired.

With a sarcastic laugh followed by a smile, he emphasised his earlier statement. "Honestly I don't know her. I just met her on the road last night and we spent the night together, but honestly I don't even know her." He raised his two-litre juice drink and took a good gulp.

"And what is the story with this drink?" I threw in another enquiry.

"This is to help me with the hangover – we had a lot to drink last night," he said. "And I'm a bit uncomfortable with her continually calling me Sweetie. I don't want to find myself with a wedding ring yet," he finished off with a laugh.

"Yes, but she looked very genuine, and when I picked you up I thought you guys were husband and wife," I responded.

"No, it was just one-night of fun, and that's it."

From there I decided not to ask any further questions as it would seem like an unnecessary invasion of privacy. I decided to change the subject and commended him for the intake of the breakfast juice as the best remedy for hangover.

Like the lady did previously, from there he took over the GPS again and started instructing me to follow his desired route to the last destination. Our drive since we dropped the lady had been from Kelmscott to just past the Armadale Hospital and entrance on Albany Highway southbound. We cruised past Kelmscott and Mt Nasura, past the BP service station on the right. As we passed the BP, he instructed me to turn right at the Albany Highway and South Western Highway intersection.

As instructed, I turned right, and he directed me into the Armadale Shopping Centre car park.

We drove past Harvey Norman, through the roundabouts, past the Police Station on the right and then turned right into the shopping complex car park. A few swings in the car park then he asked me to stop.

"Yes, I'm fine, mate, I will drop here." He pulled himself up and out of the car, still with the juice carefully clasped in his right index finger, and off he staggered.

To my amazement, what and where he was going, I need not ask, but just moved on with my driving duties.

Limping on the Road

The clock struck 4:45 am. I was travelling along Ranford Road in Canning Vale eastbound, just past the Canning Vale markets, over the rail bridge and down the hill on that bushy section illuminated by the glare of dawn. Just as I was going past the dirt road to the Rubbish Tip, casually cruising at a steady speed of about 60 kph, I saw a figure partially hidden by the shrubs on the walkway heading towards Livingstone Shopping Centre.

The road and the walkway are about five metres apart. I slowed down, cast a more concentrated glance around, and saw he was an adult male dressed in short trousers and limping with one hand on his knee. His other hand gave me the 'Please stop' signal. I kept crawling forward and did not want to risk listening to his story and ending up stuck with him in my car. I have heard so many tragedies occurring as a result of such kindness. So, my alertness level shot up!

Thirty or fifty meters past the person, I suddenly changed my mind and stopped. My inner self convinced me to hear his story and help if it was within my capacity. If it was a life and death case, then I would pick him up. Instantly I chucked the car in reverse and rolled back to the point I saw him limping forward. I stopped close to him, clearly noticing that he could not even run or walk faster to the car. I waited till he limped up to the car to present his story. As he came closer, I gave him closer scrutiny, taking in everything about him, everything on him. My imagination stretched to the contents of his pockets and anything under garments. I paid attention to any signs of protrusions as he wobbled closer. On the final limp, he clung for balance on the car roof and lowered his body to speak to me. I then slightly lowered my passenger side window, just enough space to hear each other. Straight away he inquired, "Are you Uber?" with a clear look of despair and exhaustion.

"Yes," I replied.

"Please pick me and drop me just over the hill at Livingston Shopping Centre, but I don't have any money. Please."

I focused on his face and body language.

"Something has just happened to me and I don't even know who did it. I can't recall anything. I got kicked out of the train station platform and I fell asleep. When they woke me up, I was in this shape," he explained, showing me his roughly bruised arms and legs.

The exposed parts of his body were white, pale and goose-pimpled from the early morning chill. His left arm was stuck in an off-white dirty sock clung to his chest like he was shielding his heart from excessive cold. He showed me the bruises again all over his legs, swollen knees and the cuts on his hand, this time with an exaggerated plea to win my sympathy.

In a very distressed voice, he told me that his bum was this swollen (demonstrating the damage with his cupped hands). I believed what he said and most of all, I felt sorry for him.

"OK, that's fine. Get in the car and let's go," I said, and he got in and off I drove to Livingston Shopping Centre as requested.

During that short distance trip, he kept showering me with appreciation for kind-heartedness. All he could do was wish me well and for something good to happen to me in return for the help I was offering him.

As nice as it appeared to him, I must admit that deep down I had a feeling that this was a very risky good Samaritan-ship on my part. When he came into the car with one of his hands concealed in a sock, not a glove, I had raised my eyebrows.

When he told me of his circumstances, I felt for him and all I could think of was to give him a hand. Throughout the short journey, I imagined a situation where he could start attacking me. As innocent as I was, I did not have any form of weapon or anything for self-defence in the car. I was very much aware of the level of risk I was exposing myself to.

Lucky enough, his request was genuine and throughout the trip all he kept saying was 'Thank you,' and wishing to go, rest and recover from the bruises on his body.

We safely arrived. I dropped him at one of the service stations at Livingston Shopping Centre at a very clear open spot, but there was no one around. We said our farewells and he climbed out, shook my hand and once more wished me luck (Karma). He limped up the empty Livingston Shopping Centre and disappeared in the cold morning breeze and I proceeded with my driving task.

And that rounds off Series 2. As this book went to print, the whole world is at standstill. Covid-19 has unleashed untold havoc throughout the globe.

Rideshare driving is in tatters as of now. I am not planning to keep driving when this current status is over.

However, I have a ready compilation of more to come out as Series 3. This time Series 3 will come as a full single encounter narration. Series 1 and 2 gave a list of individual stories and Series 3 will be a single hilarious, entertaining and mind-boggling encounter narrated as it happened.

The array of people and circumstances that form the experience is worth documenting. It is pleasant to hear them in story form, as an encounter, as a near miss, as a clutch of personalities or as a tale of survival.

It will be my almost gratitude if the narrations in these, so far, two series could inspire someone out there to self-challenge and do some project you have always thought about and hesitated to start. I have my own profession and drive rideshare as a side income generation. Instead of just driving I build stories from the experience. The stories are all that is in the series, true as they happened but names are totally disguised. That's me – what are you doing ... start your own, self-challenge!!

Covid-19 has brought fear and an ugly twist to our normal life, the common and simple freedom to jump into a Rideshare vehicle and go anywhere you want just vanished in a flash. Its comeback will be a bang that will be literally displayed and fully explained in Series 3. For now, enjoy Series 2.

www.ingramcontent.com/pod-product-compliance
Lightning Source LLC
Chambersburg PA
CBHW071501080526
44587CB00014B/2174